ILEA

Research and Statistics Branch Library

HMI

Routledge Education Books

Advisory editor: John Eggleston
Professor of Education
University of Warwick

HMI

Denis Lawton
and
Peter Gordon

Routledge & Kegan Paul
London and New York

First published in 1987 by
Routledge & Kegan Paul Ltd
11 New Fetter Lane, London EC4P 4EE

Published in the USA by
Routledge & Kegan Paul Inc.
in association with Methuen Inc.
29 West 35th Street, New York, NY 10001

Set in 10/11 pt Times
by Columns of Reading
and printed in Great Britain
by Billings & Sons Ltd, Worcester

British Library Cataloguing in Publication Data
Lawton, Denis
  H M I.
  1. Great Britain. Department of Education
  and Science. Inspectorate of Schools
  – History
  I. Title   II. Gordon, Peter, 1927-
354.410085'1   LB2845
ISBN 0–7102–0604–6

Contents

Preface   vii
Abbreviations   ix

Introduction: HMI today   1

1	The first hundred years (1839–1939)	7
2	HMI since the Second World War	22
3	Influence on primary schools	30
4	Influence on secondary schools	48
5	Influence on further, higher and teacher education	66
6	Women inspectors	86
7	Relations between DES, HMI and LEAs	102
8	HMI as a profession	115
9	The role of Senior Chief Inspector	127
10	The Rayner Report (1983)	141
11	Summary and conclusions	150
	Appendix I HMI: Some significant dates	156
	Appendix II Numbers of HMI (1839–1985)	163
	Appendix III DES Organization at January 1985	164

Bibliography   165
Index   174

Preface

This has been a difficult book to write. HMI plays a very important part within the English education system, and we wanted to describe this role and to relate the present to the past to show how Her Majesty's Inspectorate has changed as an institution. This book is not, however, intended as a definitive history of HMI, which would have to be a much longer and very different book; nor is it intended to be an exhaustive account of HMI as a collection of individuals, or a survey of exactly how they spend their time.

What we wanted to produce was a brief, evaluative study of a unique and important professional group. To achieve this we have relied largely on published materials, but we have also supplemented these secondary sources by unearthing hitherto unpublished documents in the Public Record Office and elsewhere.

We have also benefited greatly from talking to a number of HMI, past and present, who were all very conscious of the Official Secrets Act. Some of the assertions made about HMI and their influence must be regarded as conjecture rather than fact.

We would also wish to acknowledge the assistance given by members of the University of London Institute of Education Library and the Department of Education and Science Library, particularly Michael Humby and Arabella Wood, who drew our attention to a number of interesting publications. Finally, we would like to thank Sue Bailey, Joyce Broomhall and Beverley Jackson for their help in preparing the manuscript for publication.

Abbreviations

ACSET	Advisory Committee on Supply and Education of Teachers
AFE	Advanced Further Education
APU	Assessment of Performance Unit
ATO	Area Training Organization
CATE	Council for the Accreditation of Teacher Education
CI	Chief Inspector
CNAA	Council for National Academic Awards
CVCP	Committee of Vice-Chancellors and Principals of the Universities of the United Kingdom
DES	Department of Education and Science
DI	Divisional Inspector
DPO	Department Planning Organization
FE	Further Education
FEU	Further Education Unit
FHE	Further and Higher Education
HE	Higher Education
HMI	Her Majesty's Inspectors or Inspectorate
INSET	In-Service Education and Training
LEA	Local Education Authority
M to I	Memorandum to Inspectors
MSC	Manpower Services Commission
OECD	Organization for Economic Co-operation and Development
PAR	Programme Analysis and Research
PSG	Policy Steering Group
RI	Reporting Inspector
RSG	Rate Support Grant
RSI	Regional Staff Inspector

Abbreviations

SCI	Senior Chief Inspector
SI	Staff Inspector
TVEI	Technical and Vocational Education Initiative
UCET	Universities Council for the Education of Teachers
UDE	University Department of Education
UGC	University Grants Committee
YOP	Youth Opportunities Programme
YTS	Youth Training Scheme

Introduction

HMI today

As an institution, Her Majesty's Inspectorate of Schools (HMI) is unique. No other country possesses a group of professional educational advisers who operate independently from the controlling central authority – the Department of Education and Science (DES). HMI has a different status from the civil servants at the DES, partly because Inspectors are professional educationists and partly because they are appointed, for historical reasons, by Order of the Queen in Council – on the recommendation of the Secretary of State. HM Inspectors are an extremely influential professional group. But their position is much misunderstood: their role is often confused with that of advisers and inspectors employed by Local Education Authorities (LEAs); their relationship to the DES is complex and ambiguous; their much proclaimed independence has frequently been challenged; on several occasions the need for their continued existence has been questioned.

As with many other British institutions, HMI can only be fully understood if put into an historical context. In order to appreciate the work of HMI today it will be necessary to know how and why they were established in 1839; how their role changed during the second half of the nineteenth century; why they sank into semi-obscurity during the early years of the twentieth century; how they emerged as part of the 1944 reforms, but again faded in significance; and finally why they have been revitalized in the 1970s and 1980s.

Details of those historical factors will follow in later chapters. In this Introduction we will concentrate on a brief outline description and analysis of HMI today.

The structure and organization of HMI is often not well known even among teachers and other educationists. There are many popular misconceptions: not all HMI have their office base in the DES headquarters in Elizabeth House in London – the vast majority are stationed in one of the seven regions. Her Majesty's Inspectors of Schools are not simply concerned with schools or even with inspection: they are also concerned with further and higher education, as well as with the Youth Service and adult education; they are concerned with policy development as well as maintaining standards by means of inspection.

The present structure of the HMI in England is headed by a Senior Chief Inspector (SCI) who is responsible to the Secretary of State for Education and Science. Reporting to the SCI on a national basis are seven Chief Inspectors (CI) based in Elizabeth House, and seven Divisional Inspectors (DI) in charge of HMI activities in their regions. There are also about sixty Staff Inspectors (SI), some of whom are based in Elizabeth House.

The HMI senior management team (SCI plus seven CI)

The seven Chief Inspectors are responsible to the SCI, Mr Eric Bolton, for the co-ordination of the Inspectorate's work in the following fields (June 1986):

1 Curriculum, LEA inspections, independent schools, Services education, European and expatriate schools.
2 Secondary education.
3 Establishment and planning matters for HMI, TVEI, and Information Technology.
4 Education in the nursery, infant, junior, and middle years.
5 Vocational and technical education in further and higher education.
6 Adult and continuing education, youth and community, special needs in schools and further and higher education, ethnic minorities, and educational disadvantage.
7 General further and higher education, including teacher education and training.

National structure

In addition to the seven Chief Inspectors there are about sixty Staff Inspectors who have national responsibilities of three kinds: for *subjects* such as English or engineering; for particular *aspects* of education such as special educational needs; or for *phases* such as primary education.

In January 1985 there were 460 HMI in England, including the senior Inspectors mentioned above. In Wales, at the same time, there were 54 HMI on loan to the Welsh Office, led by a Chief Inspector, assisted by 7 Staff Inspectors. They report to the Secretary of State for Wales. Similarly, there are HMI in Scotland who report to the Scottish Education Department, not to the Secretary of State for Education and Science. No attempt will be made in this book to describe the work of HMI in Wales or Scotland.

The Senior Chief Inspector is responsible for the activities of the Inspectorate as a whole and for expressing its corporate views. He is also responsible for assigning HMI to their specific duties. The SCI and the seven Chief Inspectors deal jointly with matters concerning the whole education system outside universities. HMI inspect adult education classes, including those run by universities, and, by invitation, HMI also visit university departments of education. Much of the work of HMI is thus essentially local rather than national. To ensure adequate coverage of the whole country, England is divided into seven divisions each headed by a Divisional Inspector (DI).

Regional (divisional) structure (seven Divisional Inspectors)

DI Northern Division based in Pudsey
DI North Western Division based in Manchester
DI Midland Division based in Birmingham
DI Eastern Division based in Cambridge
DI Metropolitan and S. Midland Division based in London: William Blake House
DI Southern Division based in Croydon
DI South Western Division based in Bristol

The seven Divisional Inspectors (DI) are responsible for the work of Inspectors in the Divisions (see map). The DES does not have regional officers, and to some extent HMI act as the local agents of the DES.

Divisional Inspectors consult with Chief Inspectors and Staff Inspectors in arranging the territorial assignments of all HMI, and supervise the training of newly appointed HMI who are on probation for one year. A division will have between 40 and 65

3

HMI Divisions (England)

HMI covering the required range of 'phase', 'aspect' and 'subject' expertise; for each LEA, one HMI will be nominated as district inspector for schools and another will be district inspector for further education and higher education. They are an essential part of contact with LEAs and facilitate communication in both directions.

The work of HMI

The essential role of HMI is to advise the Secretary of State for Education and his Department. In practice this will usually mean the Permanent Secretary and other senior officials at the DES, although the SCI retains the right of direct access to the Secretary of State (see Appendix III). The advice given to the Secretary of State and his officials may be connected with policy-making (for example, on the criteria that might be applied in order to raise standards for teacher training courses), or of an information-providing kind which would enable the Secretary of State to come to decisions or to answer questions about what is happening in schools (for example, how much training would be necessary for the efficient transition to the new 16 plus examinations).

In the regions, HMI have a duty to maintain standards of work in schools and colleges, and to advise LEAs and individual institutions ('spreading good practice'). In addition, HMI carry out related functions such as running courses for teachers and others, producing publications and reports to help improve standards or reshape practice.

Central to all of these responsibilities is the duty of inspection. The function of inspection has not been legally defined, but will include any particular purpose specified by the Secretary of State. Inspection has, however, generally been interpreted to contain three principal elements:

1 A check on the use of public funds (the accountability function);
2 Provision of information to central government concerning the success or otherwise of the educational system, based on its independent professional judgment (the eyes and ears of the Secretary of State function);
3 Provision of advice to those responsible for the running of educational establishments (the advisory function).

In FE and non-university higher education, HMI recommend whether or not courses will be offered. Following inspection of independent schools they can recommend closure of schools which fall below acceptable standards. They also advise the Secretary of State on the closure of LEA schools under Section 12 of the Education Act 1980. It has sometimes been suggested that HMI have only advisory duties, but having the power to give some kinds of advice is very close to possessing executive control.

HMI has always been expected to use its influence and experience in suggesting improvements and stimulating development in the work of the schools and LEAs. In 1981, for the first time, HMI published the Annual Review of LEA expenditure in education, and has continued to publish similar reviews every year since then, despite a campaign by some Conservative politicians (see Chapter 2). This policy of publishing evidence which might appear to support criticisms of government policy has been the most clear demonstration of HMI autonomy in

5

recent years. The 1985 Review, for example, showed that schools were increasingly relying on parents' contributions and fund-raising activities to provide not only extra facilities but essential books and equipment. HMI can never criticize government policy as such, but they can make statements of fact which have clear implications.

Since January 1983, all HMI reports on schools and public sector institutions have been published. This has not only made the work of HMI much more visible, and sometimes controversial, but it has also involved HMI more clearly in the shaping of the educational system. In this connection Kogan (1986) refers to the work of HMI as being 'norm-setting', that is not simply maintaining standards but being concerned with the task of improving existing standards and establishing new norms. Kogan's view is, to some extent, in conflict with the opinion expressed in the Rayner Report on HMI (1982) which restricted the influence of HMI:

> HMI has no direct responsibility or powers (other than delegated powers for advanced course approval in higher and further education) except the right of access to institutions and the duty to inspect on behalf of the Secretary of State. It is not responsible for decisions about the organisation or the curriculum of schools: nor for standards; nor the standard of premises, equipment, staffing or other resources; nor for the deployment or promotion or appointment of teachers (para.1.12(iv)).

Clearly it is necessary for HMI responsibilities to be carefully defined so that inspectors are neither too powerful nor too weak. But if they were weakened to any considerable extent, then the balance of power and influence within the central authority would be seriously distorted. Without HMI there would be no professional group existing nationally to restrain the activities of politicians and civil servants. An important role for HMI is to prevent the politicization of education.

One purpose of this book is to provide an explanation – partly historical – of how HMI developed to reach its present unique position. Chapter 1 will provide a brief historical account up to 1939, and Chapter 2 will take the story on into the 1980s. Chapters 3 and 4 will deal in more detail with the influence of HMI on primary and secondary education, and Chapter 5 will deal with FE, HE and teacher training. The remaining five chapters will then be concerned with more specific aspects of HMI influence.

Chapter 1

The first hundred years (1839–1939)

Inspection of elementary schools

At the beginning of the nineteenth century, elementary schools, where they existed, were in the hands of religious organizations. In 1833 John Roebuck MP, asked the House of Commons to consider 'the means of establishing a system of national education'. The scheme proposed by Roebuck was so complex and ambitious that it was not accepted by the Commons, and even if passed would certainly have been rejected by the House of Lords. But there was a good deal of support in the Commons for making some provision for the education of the poor, and less than three weeks later Lord Althorp, Chancellor of the Exchequer, included in the Report of the Committee of Supply a sum not exceeding £20,000 'to be issued in aid of private subscriptions for the erection of school houses, and for the education of the children of the poorer classes in Great Britain'. This method of allocating funds had the advantage of immunity from the possibility of veto by the Lords, and although the amount of money involved was extremely small, it was a useful start to the story of state intervention in education.

In the following summer (June 1834) Roebuck, impatient at the limited progress possible under the existing arrangements, suggested a committee to enquire into an adequate system of national education. Again, Roebuck's suggestion was rejected, but a parliamentary committee was set up to examine the effect of the £20,000 grant. Several problems emerged in the Report which was published two months later: some Members were still uneasy about this kind of state interference; some were more concerned that the spending of public money should be properly supervised and controlled, and others were dissatisfied with practical aspects such as the poor quality of the teachers.

A few more years of operating this means of subsidizing schools by giving annual grants to religious societies (the National Society and the British and Foreign School Society) made the basic problem even clearer: on the one hand the money voted annually was insufficient for national needs; on the other hand it seemed improper to give bigger and bigger annual grants to the two societies without having any means of parliamentary supervision and control. In 1839 a means was found for legitimizing this annual expenditure on education; the Committee of the Privy Council on Education was established. This Committee, comprising the Lord President, the Lord Privy Seal, the Home Secretary and the Chancellor of the Exchequer, was charged with the responsibility of superintending the allocation of any money voted annually for the purpose of promoting public education. The same year the scheme was extended beyond the two religious societies and also beyond the provision of the school building to some of the running costs of the schools, although it was still assumed that most of these costs would be raised locally.

The Committee's first Secretary, Dr J.P. Kay (later Sir James Kay-Shuttleworth) drafted a minute which recommended that inspectors of schools should be appointed 'to visit schools to be henceforth aided by public money', and made the award of grants to schools conditional upon inspection. There was a good deal of opposition especially from the church to the idea of this kind of inspection, and even to the appointment of inspectors, but in December 1839, two Inspectors of schools were appointed – the Revd J. Allen and Mr H.S. Tremenheere.

It is important to note that although Allen and Tremenheere were the first HMI, they were not the first school Inspectors: Bartle (1984, p. 19) has described how the British and Foreign School Society began to develop a group of 'agents and inspectors' for their Lancastrian schools as early as 1826. The rival National Society also had representatives, including Dr. Bell himself, who regularly visited and inspected their schools. (See also Ball, 1963, Chapters 1 and 2 for an interesting comparison between HMI and other inspectorates at home and overseas in the first half of the nineteenth century; Ball is also critical of the fact that other writers on HMI have ignored the similarity of the system which developed after 1839 and the Irish system which had existed since 1820).

The part played by HMI in the development of education in the nineteenth century was of considerable importance in a number of ways. To some extent, the creation of Inspectors of Schools was based on the precedent set by inspecting factories following the Factory Acts, from 1802 onwards. The 1802 Act (the Health and Morals of Apprentices Act), for example, attempted to prevent unscrupulous mill-owners from gaining unfair advantage over more enlightened employers by worsening the conditions of work for children. Thus working hours were limited to twelve in a day, minimum standards of ventilation and hygiene were laid down, and it was specified that apprentices should receive some kind of basic instruction. Factory inspectors were appointed to enforce these regulations.

Such legislative arrangements provide an interesting example of one of the Victorian dilemmas: on the one hand the generally accepted policy in all matters affecting individuals was non-interference or laissez faire; on the other hand it was quite clear that if 'the market' operated without any kind of government intervention the result was human suffering and injustice on an enormous scale. But if the government was right to interfere in the factories why not in schools? This argument was strengthened when the government began to provide some of the money for these schools: the government needed to inspect in order to ensure that its money was being put to good use. Yet many people inside and outside Parliament had a genuine fear of government control over education and other 'private' matters. A compromise was reached: the tradition developed that HMI should not be mere functionaries but should be regarded as autonomous professionals giving their expert advice which should not be misused by politicians or civil servants. Inspectors were distrusted – particularly on the grounds of possible religious interference – but politicians and bureaucrats were distrusted even more. It was, however, necessary to issue Inspectors with clear instructions. In 1840 the instructions divided Inspectors' duties into three categories: first, to enquire into applications for grants to build or support schools; second, to inspect schools aided by grants; third, to enquire into the general condition of elementary education in particular schools. For each of those categories more detailed instructions were added.

It soon became clear that more Inspectors were needed than the two appointed in 1839. In 1850, two Assistant Inspectors were appointed; by 1852 there were twenty-four Inspectors and nine Assistant Inspectors. Many of the appointments were made on the basis of personal recommendation or through acquaintance with the Lord President. For instance, the Rev. J.J. Blandford was curate at Calne, Wiltshire, in the parish in which Lord Lansdowne's country house was situated. Matthew Arnold was also at one time Lansdowne's private secretary. Of the ninety-two Inspectors appointed between 1839 and 1870, eighty had been to Oxford or Cambridge, five to other universities, and the background of the remaining ten is unknown. None had taught in elementary schools, but most had followed careers in the church, university or in law. Just under a third had some experience of teaching in endowed or private schools (Dunford, 1981, pp. 8–23). Sutherland (1973, p. 58) suggests that at first HMI were more likely to be clergymen than of any other profession, not because they were attracted to education for religious reasons but because young men from university not knowing what to do tended either to take Orders or to go to the Bar. After the 1870 Act, however, HMI were not allowed to inspect religious teaching, and the number of Anglican clergy recruited declined dramatically.

Inspection reports

Before becoming Secretary to the Committee of the Privy Council on Education, Dr Kay had made studies of the poor in Edinburgh and Dublin, and had been Assistant Poor Law Commissioner in East Anglia and in London. He was a social reformer as well as an educational administrator. The early reports of the first Inspectors reflect a similar interest in, and concern for, the social background of the pupils attending the schools inspected. The first report issued, dated February, 1840, was written by H.S. Tremenheere and was a wide-ranging 'enquiry into the state of elementary education in the mining districts of South Wales'. This report went far beyond questions about the numbers and efficiency of schools in the area, and discussed poverty, wage rates and the trucking system, intemperance and the custom of paying out wages in public houses (Edmonds, 1965, p. 37).

This tendency to 'philosophize' rather than to inspect and report did not meet with universal approval. However C.B. Adderley, who was Vice-President of the Committee from 1858 to 1859, attempted to restrain HMI, sending back reports, objecting to some passages and asking for them to be revised. His successor, Robert Lowe, also felt that HMI should exercise restraint in their reports, and issued a minute in January 1861, stating that

> Inspectors must confine themselves to the state of the schools under their inspection and to practical suggestions for their improvement. If any report, on the judgment of their Lordships, does not conform to this standard, it is to be returned to the Inspector for revision, and if, on its being again received from him it appears to be open to the same objection, it is to be put aside as a document not proper to be printed at the public expense.

Thus it was established that if a report was thought to need revision, the Inspector who had written the report should be the one to make the necessary alterations. This was, and still is, a very important principle: in 1863 it resulted in the resignation of Robert Lowe in the midst of considerable controversy. In 1858, a Royal Commission on Education, chaired by the Duke of Newcastle, had been set up; its report recommended, *inter alia*, that greater efficiency should be achieved by examining 'every child in every school to which grants are to be paid with the view to ascertaining whether these indispensable elements of knowledge are thoroughly acquired, and to make the prospects and position of the teacher dependent to a considerable extent on the results of this examination'. Robert Lowe translated this general recommendation into a specific code, which even after some modification, amounted to the much-criticized system of 'payment by results'. Some of the severest critics of the Revised Code of 1862 were the HMI themselves, including Matthew Arnold. Opposition to the Code continued within Parliament in 1863, and Lord Robert Cecil moved a resolution complaining about the alteration of Inspectors' reports by the Department. Whilst Lowe was denying this allegation, an altered report was being circulated in the House. The government was defeated and Lowe resigned (Sylvester, 1974, p. 10). Although it is clear that Lowe did not know that the Inspector's report had been altered by one of the clerks in the Department, the drama of the resignation served to strengthen the tradition that documents written by HMI could not be changed by politicians or by their civil servants.

The events of 1862 surrounding the Revised Code were important in other respects. In order to implement payment by results, even more Inspectors were required, and their power was undoubtedly increased; but the role of the Inspector was changed in an undesirable way – away from adviser to tester and enforcer of the Code. Perhaps the most famous of all HMI, Matthew Arnold, was particularly critical of the damage being done to education by this Revised Code and payment by results. But not all HMI agreed with him (see Dunford, 1980, p. 19 for an analysis of HMI views and also Appendix 1 of this book).

The role of HMI

The influence of the Inspectorate was further increased by successive Education Acts. The Forster Act of 1870 was the basis of a national system of elementary schools, effectively filling the gaps which it was increasingly obvious that the religious bodies could not fill themselves. Whereas the early HMI had been appointed to inspect only church schools of a particular denomination, after 1870 HMI worked in all the elementary schools in a specific region. In 1871 eight Senior Inspectors were appointed in charge of divisions, and each division contained eight to ten districts. By now the Inspectorate consisted of eight Senior Inspectors, eighty-two District Inspectors, and seventy-six Assistant Inspectors. Assistant Inspectors were of a much inferior social status to the HMI they served: Assistants were drawn from the ranks of elementary school teachers and were selected by HMI on grounds of teaching skills and education. Although they performed very similar duties to HMI, their salaries were considerably lower, and they were not allowed to endorse certificates or sign reports (Sutherland, 1973, p. 78). They could never expect promotion to the rank of HMI, but in 1882 the position of Sub-Inspector was created so that some of the more senior Assistants could be rewarded (Sutherland, 1973, p. 75).

The role of HMI had been seriously distorted by the Revised Code of 1862. This system of payment by results which involved routine examining according to specific 'standards' made the Inspectors feared and hated in the elementary schools rather than welcomed as advisers, as they often had been previously. Payment by results was modified throughout the late 1860s, the 1870s and 1880s, but the damage had been done to the image of HMI. Mary Sturt examined complaints by teachers quoted in the *Schoolmaster* in the 1880s and 1890s. The general picture of HMI, even allowing for bias and exaggeration, is far from being a favourable one:

The inspector's power of annoyance did not end with the regulations. His conduct of the examination could make all the difference to the children's success. His manner might be terrifying. He could choose passages for dictation which contained words quite outside the children's vocabulary, or he could deliberately exploit the difficulties of the English language. One man would set passages from *The Times* for older scholars, and the Rev. D. J. Stewart, the most hated of the inspectors, confused the six year old infants of Greenwich with the sentence: 'if you twist that stick so long it will make your wrist ache'. Another used a passage which began 'While Hugh was culling yew, his ewes'. (Sturt, 1967, p. 351)

It would be wrong to suggest that all, or even most, HMI behaved in this way, but the evidence is that the 1862 Code had intensified the hostility between teachers and HMI. Dunford (1980, p. 81), however, suggests that Inspectors continued to champion teachers throughout the 1860s (although they were not totally uncritical before 1862). It is also interesting to note that although Inspectors had secured the privilege of uncensored reports, they were not completely free from political influence. H.E. Boothroyd (1923, p. 30), himself an HMI, reminds us that in the year 1878 when the Imperial idea was very prominent, HMI received the following instructions about 'Empire knowledge' from the Vice-President, Viscount Sandon:

attention should be specially directed to the interesting stories of history, to the lives of noble characters, and to incidents which tend to create a patriotic feeling of regard for their country and its position in the world; and while they should be made acquainted with the leading historical incidents which have taken place in their own neighbourhood, and with its special geographical features, an interest should be excited in the Colonial and Foreign Possessions of the British Crown.

Inspectors were, from the beginning, also expected to account for their time and movements to 'the Office'. The main check was made by means of official diaries in which Inspectors recorded daily how they spent their time. These diaries were sent every week to the Secretary. The 'official diary' is still used by HMI, both as an instrument of accountability and as a justification for the payment of expenses.

The South Kensington Inspectors

Although the origins of the Inspectorate must be traced back to the 1833 grant and the development of elementary schools, it would be incorrect to see the whole of the early history of HMI developing in the context of elementary education. The other major strand in the history of the Inspectorate might be referred to as the Science and Art Department or South Kensington link.

One of the problems of the elementary schools was that their functions were defined by the Codes in a very limited way. It is a gross over-simplification to suggest that the curriculum consisted of no more than the three Rs, since many schools provided a much richer programme, but in most schools the range of the curriculum was extremely limited – too limited, it was considered by many politicians and employers, to meet the needs of industry. Two years after the first grant for elementary school buildings in 1833, a House of Commons Select Committee had been set up to enquire into extending knowledge of the Arts and the principles of Design. The Committee recommended in 1836 the establishment of Schools of Design. In 1837, the Board of Trade set up a Council of the Government Schools of Design including the Vice-President of the Board of Trade and a number of Royal Academicians to supervise the 'Central School', which opened in June 1837, in Somerset House. A number of teachers for Art and Design were trained, and in 1841, Schools of Design were established in a number of provincial towns, usually staffed by a teacher trained at the Central School. In 1842 it was decided that in order to guide the development of the provincial Schools of Design, the Director of the Central School should act as Inspector and be paid a fee and expenses for each visit to a provincial school.

In 1843, however, the two positions were separated and the director of the Central School resigned his post and became an occasional Inspector. In 1850, the first full-time appointment of an Inspector for Higher Education was made by the Committee of Council for Trade: not, it should be noted, by the Queen in Council, so he should not be referred to as one of 'Her Majesty's Inspectors'.

Despite the appointment of a full-time Inspector, the Schools of Design were not regarded as satisfactory. One of the more vocal critics was Henry Cole, who was later to have an opportunity to effect a number of changes. After the Great

Exhibition of 1851 there was a good deal more discussion about the need to encourage industrial skills. In 1852, a Department of Practical Art was established by the Board of Trade, with Henry Cole as General Superintendent; and in 1853, a Science Division was added. The Science and Art Department, as it was known, was eventually (1856) situated in South Kensington and began administering parliamentary grants for the teaching of science and art on a considerable scale, initially quite independently of the Committee of the Privy Council on Education. Henry Cole and Lyon Playfair were joint Secretaries, the former being Inspector for Art and the latter acting also as Inspector for Science.

Lyon Playfair left the Department of Science and Art in 1858, and was succeeded as Inspector by Captain J.F.D. Donnelly seconded from the Royal Engineers. Donnelly never returned to military duties, but remained with the Department for the rest of his career, becoming Director of Science in 1874, and Secretary of the Science and Art Department in 1884; by 1887 he had also reached the military rank of Major-General, and was knighted in 1893 (Armytage, 1950, p. 15).

In 1856 the Department of Science and Art had been transferred from the Board of Trade to the Education Department, and after 1859 general grants became available for the promotion of science and art in schools. These were allocated by Donnelly and his colleagues on the basis of payment by results of the 'South Kensington Examinations', thus anticipating the payment by results of the 1862 Revised Code by several years. In both cases payment by results was administered by Inspectors acting as examiners. Despite the volume of work in the Science and Art Department, by 1872 there were still only two permanent Inspectors, but from 1876 to 1890 there were four, all of whom were extremely well qualified in either science or art; in addition, a number of officers from the Royal Engineers were used as part-time Inspectors.

In 1881, the Royal Commission of Technical Instruction (Samuelson) was set up and it reported in 1882 and 1884. A number of important suggestions were made, including the recommendation that there should be more practical instruction in elementary and secondary schools. Although the elementary school curriculum was subject to the Codes which strictly defined what an education grant should be spent on, some school boards had set up higher grade schools financed from science and art grants. The Technical Instruction Act of 1889 enabled counties and county boroughs to levy a rate for technical education; this opportunity was enhanced by the Local Taxation (Customs and Excise) Act of 1890 which transferred to local authorities quite large sums of 'whiskey money' which could be spent on technical education. Technical education was defined very broadly by the Science and Art Department and by their Inspectors, to such an extent that some suggested that only classics was excluded from their responsibilities.

All these developments increased the workload of the South Kensington Inspectors. In 1892, A.H.D. Acland became Vice-President of the Committee of Council on Education, and one of his reforms was the re-organization of the Science and Art Inspectors: he appointed a number of new Inspectors who were not only very competent in their subject specialism, but had also had teaching experience. These Science and Art Inspectors were sometimes referred to as 'Acland's twelve apostles' (although there were thirteen in all if the one responsible for Ireland was included with the two for Scotland and the ten for England and Wales). Their duties were very extensive: they were responsible for the supervision of grants in secondary schools, technical schools, schools of art, science and art classes in elementary schools, evening classes in science and pupil teacher centres. In addition, there were considerable numbers of acting Inspectors, usually Royal Engineers officers, and local Inspectors, who were only concerned with examining drawing in elementary schools.

There was clearly an overlap between the work of HMI and the South Kensington Inspectors, but they remained quite separate until 1901. An additional reason for the amalgamation was that in 1898 Science and Art examinations were abolished, and when that happened some of the South Kensington Inspectors (but none of the Royal Engineers officers) were transferred to the elementary branch. Before transfer in 1901, however, Acland's re-organization had created a strong group of Inspectors subdivided into Divisions and Districts. In May, 1901, by an Order in Council twenty of the Science and Art Inspectors were appointed as HMI. Later some of the Science and Art Inspectors joined the Secondary Branch.

The two groups of Inspectors were now unified with the title of HMI. It should be noted that it is not correct to refer to the Science and Art Department Inspectors before 1901 as HMI, and some writers have failed to make this distinction sufficiently clear (see Chapter 8). In 1899 the Board of Education Act had also made possible the creation of a Board of Education; in January,

1900, the Duke of Devonshire became the first President of the Board. The implementation of many of the reforms referred to above soon began to take place. A tidying up of the central organization was necessary: apart from the nineteenth-century overlap between the Education Department in Whitehall and Science and Art in Kensington, the Charity Commissioners were responsible for many of the endowed grammar schools and public schools, and the Board of Agriculture made grants for various kinds of agricultural education and training. According to Lowndes (1937, p. 61) no fewer than ten members of the Cabinet were responsible for various kinds of educational institutions. The integration of the two groups of Inspectors was only one aspect of the much-needed re-organization. The full integration of Science and Art with Education was clearly essential, but may have been delayed until the retirement of Sir John Donnelly in 1899. Although the Science and Art Department had been officially transferred to the Education Department in 1856, it had continued to be based at South Kensington and had functioned in most respects as an independent body. The departure of Donnelly, after forty years' service, now made complete re-organization possible as well as desirable.

Inspecting secondary schools

The next phase in the history of HMI came after the 1902 Education Act, which made possible the development of state maintained secondary schools. Robert Morant became Permanent Secretary of the Board of Education and reorganized the central authority including HMI. The Inspectorate was reorganized into three branches: elementary, secondary and technological, each headed by a Chief Inspector. The subsidiary services of teacher training and art education were also led by a Chief Inspector. As well as the three branches organized on a national basis, there were now nine regional divisions as well as separate departments (since 1885) for Wales and Scotland. Thus the Inspectorate was beginning to resemble its present organization and structure.

The restructuring of HMI into branches (which are now referred to as 'phases') corresponded to the branches of the new Board of Education. This enabled the HMI and civil servants to work more closely in the task of implementing the many reforms and developments which followed the 1902 Education Act. HMI was becoming not simply the financial watchdogs of Parliament and the examiners of standards, but something closer to the Kay-Shuttleworth concept of the 'eyes and ears' of the central authority.

One major change was that the 1902 Act enabled the new Local Education Authorities (LEAs) to provide secondary education out of the rates. Some higher grade elementary schools and pupil teacher centres were converted into secondary schools, and a large number of new schools were also built. In 1904 the Board of Education issued Regulations for Secondary Schools, and the new secondary branch of HMI was organized to undertake the work of inspecting secondary schools; at the same time adapting to a style of inspection much less restrictive than the payment by results elementary model. Some of the new secondary HMI had been transferred from South Kensington, but there was a considerable need for more specialists in languages and other subjects. Each secondary inspector now had general duties in relation to the secondary schools in his district, but a novel feature of the work of secondary HMI was the concept of 'the full inspection' by which a school was inspected as a whole, and the financial and other aspects of school management discussed with representatives of the governing body. To some extent, therefore, the LEA was also under scrutiny as well as the teaching staff of the school, especially after the 1918 Education Act had made LEAs responsible for preparing complete schemes covering all the educational activities of their areas.

Meanwhile, the new Technological Branch of HMI did not simply continue the work of the South Kensington Inspectors, but soon became a group of experts covering the work of Evening Continuation Schools as well as the engineering, building, mining and commercial subjects taught in various institutions of technical education. They also took on responsibility for the rapidly expanding classes in politics, economics and literary subjects organized by the Workers' Educational Association and other organizations. They forged links with Chambers of Commerce and Employers' Federations in relation to their vocational and careers advisory responsibilities. In that connection they also took on responsibility in the early 1920s for intelligence testing and industrial psychology.

Medical inspections

One further development within the Inspectorate must not escape preliminary mention at this stage, and that is medical inspection. In 1893 the Elementary Education (Blind and Deaf Children) Act made authorities responsible for maintaining schools for children with those two specific defects. (We would now say 'special needs', but the nineteenth-century and early twentieth-century terminology referred to 'defective children'). Dr Alfred Eicholz was the first HMI with medical qualifications appointed to inspect the schools set up under the 1893 Act; in addition the 1899 Act permitted authorities to extend their provision to epileptic and other 'defective' children. This innovation within the Inspectorate led to two very different twentieth-century developments. First, the whole process of medical inspection, school health and welfare (including school meals), and a school health service later to be divorced from HMI and become the Medical Department of the Board of Education with its own hierarchy and a Chief Medical Officer. The second development was the section of the Inspectorate specifically concerned with special education or children with special needs.

The HMI tradition

From their origins in 1839, HMI were concerned principally with elementary education, to be the guardians of public money and to maintain minimum standards. Another important influence was that of the South Kensington Inspectors in Science and Art. The work within both traditions was seriously distorted for a while by the Victorian version of utilitarianism which gave rise specifically to payment by results and generally to a narrow view of examining rather than advising and disseminating good practice.

By the end of the nineteenth century payment by results had gradually been weakened to such an extent that it hardly existed, yet HMI still tended to be distrusted and feared by elementary teachers. The 1902 Act was a great opportunity for change. Although the 1904 Secondary Regulations have sometimes been regarded as over-prescriptive, the secondary HMI went about their task in a much less punitive way. It was also highly significant that in the year after the 1904 Secondary Regulations, the elementary Code was replaced by the Board of Education Blue Book, *Suggestions for the Consideration of Teachers and others concerned with the work of Public Elementary Schools*. The fact that everything contained in the Book including the 'specimen schemes' were suggestions was emphasized:

The only uniformity of practice that the Board of Education desire to see in the teaching of Public Elementary Schools is that each teacher shall think for himself, and work out for himself such methods of teaching as may use his powers to the best advantage and be best suited to the particular needs and conditions of the school. (p. 6)

The Handbook was revised and re-issued from time to time, and provides evidence of increasing liberalization of elementary education throughout the 1920s and 1930s. Part of the credit for the growth of a progressive ideology must go to Edmond Holmes, who was Chief Inspector for Elementary Schools from 1905–11. His publications included *What Is and What Might Be* (1911) which was published after his retirement, and reflects his experience as a reforming inspector. Holmes's thesis was that the regimentation of children remained the dominant mode of teacher behaviour long after payment by results had been abolished. Holmes criticized the teaching style which was designed to oppress the child 'to leave nothing to his nature, nothing to his spontaneous life, nothing to his free activity: to repress all his natural impulses; to drill his energies into complete quiescence; to keep his whole being in a state of sustained and painful tension' (pp. 48–9). The fact that the 1927 Handbook was, according to Selleck (1972, p. 124), more progressive than the 1905 version demonstrated that Holmes was by no means an isolated voice in the Inspectorate at that time. 'Progressivism' at least among the elementary HMI was becoming part of 'official thinking'. Other evidence for a changing attitude towards elementary education is contained in the Report of the Consultative Committee on the Primary School (1931). This was not, of course, written by HMI, but reflected the views of some of them.

Conclusion

Although the payment by results image of HMI lived on in the folk memory of teachers throughout the 1930s (and beyond), HMI were by now playing a very different role from that of examiners of standards – so different that to some their profile seemed to be too low. The obvious question was whether they were necessary at all, especially since LEAs had without exception developed their own groups of inspectors and advisers. In the post-1944 period it should have been clear that a new HMI role, one more concerned with national policy, was needed.

Chapter 2

HMI since the Second World War

The 1944 Education Act was a major educational reform which is still, in most respects, the current legislation governing the English educational system. Its achievements included the provision of universal secondary education up to the age of fifteen (and sixteen 'as soon as possible'); the abolition of fees in state maintained schools, and the end of the sharp distinction between elementary and secondary education (including teachers' salaries): after 1944 primary education from 5–11 was followed automatically by secondary 11–16. It was also reaffirmed that HMI had a right of access to educational institutions:

> It shall be the duty of the Minister to cause inspections to be made of every educational establishment at such intervals as appear to him to be appropriate, and to cause a special inspection of any such establishment to be made whenever he considers such an inspection desirable. (Section 77)

The Act was the result of discussions about education which had continued throughout the war. The preparation of a 'confidential' Green Book *Education After the War* began in 1941; HMI contributed to these discussions but were not as influential as they might have been. Gosden's (1976, p. 265) account of the Green Book's construction gives the impression that the three Chief Inspectors involved (Duckworth, Charles and Elliott), together with the Senior Woman Inspector (Miss Hammonds) were overshadowed by the very powerful civil servants at the Board, in particular S.H. Wood, G.G. Williams and R.S. Wood. Apart from the Chief Inspectors, HMI officially knew nothing about the discussions on *Education After the War* and some of them complained about being 'kept in the dark' when some of the papers were circulated to local authorities. R.S. Wood, however, refused to involve HMI to any great extent (Gosden, 1976, pp. 266–7).

Senior HMI were also involved in the process of converting the Green Book into the 1943 White Paper on Educational Reconstruction which preceded the 1944 Education Act. After the 1944 Act a Departmental Committee recommended a unified Inspectorate, an increase in numbers, the abolition of the grade of Assistant Inspector, and the appointment of three more Chief Inspectors. All the recommendations were implemented after 1945. In order to carry out satisfactorily their many new tasks, the size of the the Inspectorate was dramatically increased – from 364 in 1945 to 565 in 1950. The Permanent Secretary to the Ministry of Education at the time, Sir John Maud, considered that the pace of recruitment was probably too fast (Maud, 1981, p. 54).

HMI were also re-organized on a more coherent territorial basis. This was partly connected with the fact that the Act gave the newly created Minister of Education power to enforce the provisions of the Act in the local authorities. The idea of partnership was still strong, but the need for a degree of national uniformity in terms of educational standards was recognized; the pre-war differences between generous and parsimonious authorities were no longer considered to be compatible with post-war egalitarian ideals. HMI were to have a role in ensuring that minimum standards were observed, although this specific function was not clearly stated in the Act; the post of Divisional Inspector thus gained status, becoming more concerned with educational matters rather than administration.

The changing role of HMI

The immediate post-war period, lasting until about 1960, has been referred to as the age of optimism and consensus in education. Money spent on education was considered to be a good investment and there was a national drive to build more schools of better quality. In such times it was natural for HMI to keep a fairly low profile. In primary education they became identified with 'progressive' views of teaching methods and organization, until the Plowden Report (1967) (see Chapter 3). In secondary education the HMI view seems to have generally coincided with that of civil servants at the Ministry of Education

– namely, supporting a tripartite system of secondary schools rather than recommending comprehensive or multilateral policies. In 1959 the Senior Chief Inspector, Percy Wilson, was less cautious than usual when he told a conference of head teachers that 'after three successive Labour Party defeats at general elections the danger for grammar schools was over, and they could look forward to a long period of stability' (Fenwick, 1976, p. 127).

It would appear, however, that HMI, like their colleagues in the Ministry, gradually became converted to, or at least reconciled to, the idea of comprehensive education: by the late 1970s they were, as we shall see, advocating curriculum policies of a completely comprehensive kind. It will be important to try to identify what happened during those years – roughly 1960–75 – to produce such a significant ideological change.

Meanwhile, the low profile of HMI in the 1950s inevitably led to questions about their continued importance and even their continued existence. Having long ago lost the inquisitorial role involved in enforcing 'payment by results', it was necessary to acquire a new, less directive function, but it was by no means clear exactly what it should be. Evans (1975, p. 132), suggests that after 1944 the role of HMI was limited to guiding and assisting teachers 'by persuasion rather than dictation'. But most local authorities now had effective bodies of advisers and inspectors themselves – so what was the function of a national body of Inspectors? Were they still needed?

In 1956 it was felt necessary to have a Working Party to review the role of HMI. It was chaired by SCI, Sir Martin Roseveare, and was extremely introspective in style. No discussions were held with LEAs or other 'partners' during the deliberations of the Working Party, and little attempt was made to explain any change in practice to teachers and others afterwards. A particular problem seemed to be the possible overlap of functions with local authority inspectors and advisers. One of the recommendations of the Roseveare Committee was that the size of Her Majesty's Inspectorate should be reduced from 547 to 513, but twelve years later (when HMI were scrutinized by the 1967–8 Parliamentary Select Committee), the number of Inspectors had been reduced by only four out of a target reduction of thirty-four.

The period from 1956 to the publication of the review by the Select Committee in 1968 probably represents the lowest period of HMI influence and morale. The Select Committee was not impressed by communication within the Inspectorate where the diffusion of information was described by the Permanent Secretary as 'a bit primitive'. A complaint from HMI themselves was that there always seemed to be the danger of HMI recommendations 'getting lost', presumably if the senior civil servants did not like them. And the problem of overlap between HMI and local authority inspectors still existed. The one positive move during the period was the establishment of the Curriculum Study Group in 1962; although this was replaced by the Schools Council in 1964, the involvement of HMI in curriculum was highly significant. However, 1968 also seemed to be a low point in terms of the independence of HMI from the Department:

> Throughout our enquiry, we heard a good deal of evidence about the independence of the Inspectorate. We do not consider appointment by Her Majesty in Council to be of any great significance, although we recognize that it 'delights the people who enjoy it.' That HMI is wholly independent of the Department is a myth: 'the Department and the Inspectorate are a very integrated body' (Report of the Select Committee on Education and Science, p. xi).

The Select Committee recommended that full scale inspections should cease, and that the number of HMI correspondingly be reduced:

> What is needed is a smaller, possibly more highly specialized Inspectorate, more closely related to its changed functions, and more in touch with special developments affecting education.

The Select Committee was critical of some aspects of the Inspectorate, but by 1968 the role of HMI was already changing, and changing in the direction of exerting much greater influence. In fact the Select Committee Report can be interpreted as being more critical of the Department than of HMI. A real weakness was that the Department did not use the professional expertise of HMI in an effective way. It was also felt that the SCI would only be sufficiently powerful in the Civil Service hierarchy if he were promoted to the rank of Deputy Secretary.

At roughly this same time Edward Boyle, in an interview with Maurice Kogan, had also complained that not enough use was made of the professional knowledge of HMI within the Department:

> The Inspectorate has played less of a part in policy-making that I for one would have liked to see. . . . I don't think there was a

25

sufficiently strong tradition that when you had a major
discussion the Senior Chief Inspector should normally be
invited in. . . . there may have been personal reasons over the
years why this tended not to happen. But, for whatever reason,
he didn't play a big enough part in policy-making in the
Department, whoever he was (Boyle and Crosland, 1971,
pp. 130–1).

But during the early 1970s, significant changes were taking
place which were to revitalize HMI, and radically alter the role of
HMI, especially in their relations with the Department (and we
should note that Edward Boyle was referring to earlier periods of
service at the Ministry of Education, namely, 1957–9 and
1962–4). In 1967, the Planning Branch was established in which
civil servants were supplemented by the expertise of economists
and statisticians, but HMI were only involved in a marginal way.
In 1970, however, the change of government coincided with the
arrival of a new Permanent Secretary, Sir William Pile; the
Planning Branch was replaced by a Department Planning
Organization (DPO) and a new system of Programme Analysis
and Research (PAR) was adopted. An important part of the new
system was the existence of the Policy Steering Group (PSG),
chaired by the Permanent Secretary; a significant feature of the
new system was that the SCI (now promoted to Deputy Secretary
rank) became an *ex-officio* member of this key committee which
was concerned with guiding the planning of educational policy.
The crucial work of PSG was directly supported by Policy Group
A (concerned with higher, further and adult education) and
Policy Group B (schools and 16–19), each of which included the
appropriate Chief Inspector as a member. Each of these policy
groups was in turn supported by more specialized sub-groups on
which the relevant Staff Inspectors automatically served. The
importance of an efficient committee structure replacing informal
communication systems where HMI ideas could 'get lost' should
not be underestimated.

HMI and education planning

It is sometimes suggested that the DES began to take planning
seriously, and to make better use of HMI in that process, only
after 1976 when the Department was criticized by both the
Organization for Economic Co-operation and Development and

the Parliamentary Expenditure Committee. The evidence is, however, that measures had been taken to improve planning several years before those two critical reports were published. A much more positive participation by HMI in educational planning was initiated by H.W. French (SCI, 1972–4), and continued vigorously by Sheila Browne (SCI, 1974–83).

The Reports of OECD (1975) and the Expenditure Committee (1976) were, however, critical of the DES. The OECD experts examined the 1972 White Paper as a piece of policy-making; the DES was accused of being more concerned to minimize controversiality, and of confusing policy with resource allocation. The Expenditure Committee Report was concerned with 'policy-making in the DES'. The two main complaints were that the DES was excessively secretive and that it lacked an adequate planning organization. As we noted above, measures had already been taken to improve policy studies at the DES by 1976, but the publication of the two reports in the same year undoubtedly stimulated the DES into a more open stance in policy-making.

Since 1976 both the DES and HMI have advocated a greater degree of central planning in education, including more control over the curriculum. In 1976 the Prime Minister, James Callaghan, made the famous Ruskin speech and launched the 'Great Debate'. In the same year the 'confidential' Yellow Book was leaked to the Press. Fred Mulley, Secretary of State for Education in 1975, had been asked by the Prime Minister to produce a report on the current state of educational standards; the DES (presumably with the co-operation of HMI) produced a report which was critical of progressive methods in primary schools and the typical curricular arrangements in secondary schools. The critical remarks in the document provided a springboard for a more directive policy on the curriculum by DES in the late 1970s and early 1980s. In particular the criticisms of the Schools Council were used to secure the eventual closure of the Schools Council, thus leaving curriculum influence clear for DES and HMI.

Curriculum planning

In 1977, a very important document on the curriculum was published by HMI. It was called *Curriculum 11 to 16* (sometimes referred to as the Red Book) and set out to propose a curriculum based not on subjects but on 'areas of experience'; option schemes for the 14–16 age group were criticized for failing to produce a balanced curriculum; instead a common curriculum plan 11–16 was advocated. A later document, *Curriculum 11 to 16: Towards a Statement of Entitlement* (1983f) suggests that the group of HMI responsible began to work together in 1975, but the HMI interest in curriculum theory and curriculum planning began even earlier, and took on a planning role in 1974 when Sheila Browne became SCI. Schools Council Working Paper 33 provides an interesting account of the Scarborough Conference (1969) on the whole curriculum, from which it is clear that HMI were already discussing theoretical aspects of curriculum planning in the late 1960s.

> One group, in defining the curriculum, was moving towards considerations of this kind, while an HMI representative pointed out that there was a group in the Inspectorate already giving it serious thought. He defined the essentials of a good curriculum as giving importance to personal development, aesthetic experience, experience of the material world and of society, and 'transcendentalism' – ideals and inspiration (Schools Council, 1971, p. 26).

In 1977, the Senior Chief Inspector reflected on the HMI view of curriculum in an address to the Council for Local Education Authorities (CLEA). She claimed that HMI had a critical rather than an initiating role to play in curriculum planning. But in fact since 1977 HMI have been increasingly active in policy-making in curriculum matters. The HMI curriculum group followed up *Curriculum 11 to 16* (1977) with a joint study with five LEAs in which the areas of experience model was discussed and tried out in a number of schools (DES, 1981 and 1983). In 1985, a new series of publications called *Curriculum Matters* covering the whole of the curriculum 5–16 was started. These have been influential in the process of schools re-examining their own curriculum planning.

Surveys and reports

During the 1970s another important change in HMI work was initiated. Reports on individual schools ceased to be regarded as unique studies to be filed away, but were collected together systematically and used as the basis of survey reports which took on the status of influential policy documents. The survey of primary schools, published as *Primary Education in England* (DES, 1978), was a very important example; and this was followed by the secondary survey *Aspects of Secondary Education in England* (DES, 1979b) and several others. In addition, HMI made notable contributions to such important policy reports as *A Language for Life* (DES, the Bullock Report, 1975).

In 1983 the decision was taken by the Secretary of State for Education that all HMI reports should be published (except those on university departments of education which were technically 'visits' rather than inspections – see Chapter 5). Meanwhile, HMI had been submitted to its most searching scrutiny. Sir Derek Rayner (later Lord Rayner) was asked to include HMI in a series of reviews of government departments; the report was published in 1982. A summary of the Rayner recommendations will be included in Chapter 10. At this stage it is sufficient to say that the report was generally favourable, and that HMI were confirmed and strengthened in their existing role – despite, it is alleged, the hope strongly expressed by the Prime Minister, Margaret Thatcher, that more radical changes would be suggested including a return to an inquisitorial role.

Another important development in HMI activities has been the publication since 1981 of Annual Surveys of LEAs' expenditure. Each year HMI have provided evidence to show that low spending tends to coincide with inadequate provision of teaching services. In 1984 (and possibly other years) HMI were under considerable pressure from Conservative Party politicians to moderate or suppress such evidence. It is a tribute to the independence of HMI that such pressure was resisted, and reports on LEA expenditure have continued to be published annually. This will be further discussed in Chapter 7.

Conclusion

During the forty years following the Second World War, the significance and status of HMI first slumped to a low point in the 1960s, but then, by adapting to the changing educational environment in the 1970s and 1980s, they not only overcame this difficulty but strengthened their overall position.

Chapter 3

Influence on primary schools

The end of 'payment by results'

Many of the images of HMI in the primary sector of education derive from the era of payment by results. Perhaps the best-known examples are those of Charles Dickens in *Hard Times* and Flora Thompson in *Larkrise to Candleford*, where the visit of the Inspector is depicted as an occasion which struck terror into both pupils and teachers. What should be remembered, however, is that the role of HMI as an enforcer of uniformity of curriculum and character between schools through the annual examination was for only a comparatively short period in the Inspectorate's history, lasting a little over thirty years.

The ending of payment by results from 1895 was the final acknowledgment of changes in social, political and educational attitudes. There is much evidence to show that within the Inspectorate itself there was dissatisfaction with the existing system. Matthew Arnold, for instance, pointed out that HMI, as an agency for testing and promoting the intellectual life of schools, were succeeding only in the former sphere. Another Inspector, W.P. Turnbull, deplored 'the open manipulation of the *child as a grant-earning thing*, rather than his treatment as a trust' (Turnbull, 1919, p. 139). Such views accorded well with the activities of groups of men and women who adopted many educational ideas originating either on the Continent or in the United States, and who were identified by Selleck (1968, p. 333) as practical, moral, natural, social and scientific educationists. Though these groups by no means necessarily worked together they nevertheless shared certain assumptions, particularly an opposition to instrumentary education and the system of payment by results.

Since the 1870 Education Act, changes had also taken place in the organization of elementary education itself. The Act was concerned with providing suitable schooling for the majority of the population up to the age of 13. The elementary school by name existed until the 1944 Education Act, but it was soon appreciated that there were different needs for different age groups. The first London School Board in 1871 set the pattern for urban areas by classifying infants' schools for children below seven, junior schools for those between seven and ten, and senior schools for older children. With the lengthening of compulsory school attendance following legislation in 1876 and 1880, the need for separate junior and senior departments was emphasized.

The growth in the provision of infants' education nationally from about 1875 and the successful adoption of new teaching methods led to a consideration of the next stage, the six- to nine-year-old group. From 1894 onwards, the Education Department in its 'Instructions to Inspectors' drew attention to the fact that the work and teaching methods employed with this group were the least satisfactory part of the system. This situation can be accounted for in a number of ways. Only a few of the larger Boards had appointed supervisors of younger children, the Codes made few concessions for younger children and perhaps most importantly, hardly any HMI had had any direct experience of elementary school teaching. Signs of official encouragement of a more flexible approach by the Department were evident, for instance, in Circular 322 of 1893, addressed to Inspectors, in the 1894 Instructions. This was a long and detailed document on the instruction of infants in Froebelian theory and practice (Whitbread, 1972, p. 48). Another significant advance was the appointment of two women Inspectors in 1895–6 to help in the inspection of girls and young children in elementary schools. Their influence was much greater than their numerical strength, as will be shown in Chapter 6.

The new freedom given to schools from 1895 was described by the Education Department two years later: 'It has been our aim to remove, as far as possible, all restrictions which might unduly hamper the freedom of teachers and managers in their desire to increase the efficiency of the schools and to promote the welfare of the scholars' (Committee of Council on Education, Report

1897–8, p. xv). The implications of this new approach were made clear by the Department in its Instructions for Inspectors, issued in 1898:

> Inspection should not include any of the processes hitherto employed in formal examination. The inspection of a school . . . consists chiefly in the observation of methods pursued by the teacher, and any questioning that may be employed should be confined to the purpose of ascertaining how far these methods have been successful.

Annual Inspection, with formal notice to the managers at least ten days in advance, was replaced by 'surprise visits', i.e. unannounced visits to a school by HMI for a day or half day. Later, following the procedures established by the Secondary Inspectorate after 1905, the full inspection was used (see Chapter 4) though patterns of visiting and reporting varied from district to district.

Another important change was reflected in the way in which HMI attempted to influence the curriculum of the elementary school. For many years after the New Code of 1882 had been promulgated, it was customary for the Education Department (and later the Board of Education) to issue with the Instructions to Inspectors specimen schemes of elementary school work. These represented an official interpretation of the annual code itself, and increasingly took on the character of a compendium of suggestions and advice for teachers. However, in 1904 the Code was issued in a modified form, the Instructions were withdrawn and the Board promised to 'issue shortly a companion volume to the Code containing various suggestions for the consideration of those who came into contact with the scholars in elementary schools, and are concerned with the educational as distinct from the administrative aspects of schools life'.

This Code followed the transfer of responsibility for the maintenance and control of elementary schools to the new LEAs created by the 1902 Education Act. Many ex-elementary school heads were being recruited as local Inspectors, and advice from the centre would be welcomed by them. It was with the wider audience in mind that in August 1905 the promised publication appeared, in the form of a government Blue Book entitled *Suggestions for the Consideration of Teachers and Others Concerned in the Work of Public Elementary Schools* (Board of Education, 1905). Although the driving force behind the publication was Morant, the overall supervision of the volume was in the hands of three people: Sir William Anson, Parliamentary Secretary, Board of Education, W.R. Davies, a Junior Examiner who carried out the editing work and Cyril Jackson, the Chief Inspector of the newly-formed Elementary School Branch.

It is clear that Jackson played a leading part in shaping the philosophy of elementary education expounded in *Suggestions*. Jackson drew on the talents of many of his distinguished colleagues who contributed chapters on different aspects of the curriculum: J.C. Iles on the teaching of arithmetic, Arthur Somervell on singing, T.G. Rooper on gardening, A. Eicholz on the health of pupils and Jackson himself on geography. Dr Frank Heath, then Director of the Office of Special Inquiries, wrote on the teaching of English, and members of the academic community and other outside experts contributed chapters (Gordon, 1985, pp. 43–4). The Preparatory Memorandum set out its main purpose, namely, to offer guidance to teachers 'and even more to encourage careful reflection on the practice of their profession'. Only a limited number of teachers was able to keep abreast of recent developments in educational matters: it was the intention in future editions of the *Suggestions* to make a continuous and systematic review of all developments which made for success in the elementary school. Stressing that 'It is not desirable to encourage the pedantry of pedagogy', the Board strongly recommended LEAs to try out experimental work in one or two selected schools; teachers were also requested to report any educational innovations carried out in their district.

The Blue Book was warmly received by the educational press and the teachers. The ten areas of the curriculum considered represented practical and enlightened approaches: examples were given of how current practices might be altered and how differences in children's abilities were to be recognized. One compliment paid to the authors, who of course were anonymous to the public, appeared in an editorial of an education journal as follows:

From the documents which formerly issued from Whitehall we were wont to infer a weird council of shrivelled wind-dried mummies, who had been sitting there from time immemorial, opening their leathern jaws at intervals and enunciating injunctions which were afterwards embodied in codes and circulars. . . . We think it probable that the members of this ghostly council have at last mouldered into dust and that their places are now occupied by human beings, some of whom, indeed, have not only caught a glimpse of children, but have had children of their own (*School Manager*, 5 August 1905, pp. 129–30).

Shortly after this triumph for the Elementary Inspectorate, Jackson retired and was replaced by a new Chief Inspector, Edmond Holmes. An Inspector of vast experience – he had become HMI in 1875 shortly after leaving Oxford – Holmes had already published two books on philosophy and several volumes of poetry, extolling the master law of Nature, that of growth and development and pleading for an alliance between thought and feeling. In a remarkable confidential letter to the President of the Board of Education, Runciman, in 1909, Holmes claimed that the education given to pupils in elementary schools was misguided: teachers were compelled to destroy the freedom, initiative and intelligence of their charges and teachers were wrong with their aims and their methods. Holmes, like Morant, attributed much of the blame to inspectors appointed by the LEAs: many of these inspectors had served under the School Board regime. 'Our Inspectors are doing their best,' Holmes told Runciman, 'too often in the teeth of opposition from Local Authorities and Local Inspectors, to bring about a better state of things. But the evil effects of 25 years of mal-administration and mal-education will not easily wear themselves out' (Holmes to Runciman, 3 February 1909, Runciman Papers, WR 44).

Holmes probably had in mind such instances as the joint report by the seven London School Board inspectors in 1901, accusing the Board of Education of being responsible, by their more enlightened policies, for a fall in efficiency in the schools, a view supported by local inspectors outside London. In June 1908, Holmes had sent round a circular addressed to each elementary District Inspector requesting full details of sex, salary and qualifications of local Inspectors. The returns were collated and analysed by Holmes and his findings were circulated in January 1910 to HMI in the form of a memorandum marked 'Strictly Confidential'. Of the 123 local inspectors (109 were men and only fourteen were women) Holmes noted that 101 were ex-elementary school teachers and of the rest only two or three had been to a public school and then Oxford or Cambridge. Of the former 'Very few of our Inspectors have a good word to say for them . . . The existence of these Inspectors stereotypes routine, perpetuates cast-iron methods and forms an effectual bar to development and progress.' Their failings, according to Holmes, were explainable by the fact 'that elementary teachers are, as a rule, uncultured and imperfectly educated, and that many – if not most – of them are creatures of tradition and routine.'

This memorandum was approved for restricted circulation by Morant and became known (incorrectly) as the Holmes-Morant Circular. The contents of the memorandum were leaked to the National Union of Teachers and following a subsequent outcry, the matter was raised in the Commons. As a result, both Morant and Runciman were transferred to other offices, though by now Holmes had retired. Nevertheless, the damage had been done and the relationship between HMI and local inspectors was soured. The exposure of the memorandum was perhaps a particularly suitable vehicle for expressing long-standing grievances by teachers and inspectors on the nature and content of elementary school education. As Eaglesham (1953, p. 108) stated,

> The seeds of the crisis were sown in the 1870 Elementary Education Act. Those who framed the Act did not define 'elementary'. They did not co-ordinate it with other forms of education. They did not prescribe the scope of the Act's operation. None of the planners of subsequent legislation and none of the administrators grappled with this fundamental omission.

Before discussing the ways in which the elementary Inspectors were affected by the newer freedom given to teachers in schools, we must draw attention to an important constraint. Until 1926, the Board stipulated that the timetable and the curriculum, apart from religious instruction, were subject to their approval. HMI approved it on their behalf. The timetable was to be hung up conspicuously in the school and needed to bear the Inspector's signature and a certificate of approval by the LEA. Selby-Bigge, Morant's successor as Permanent Secretary, ruled that LEA consent was not absolutely necessary and many of the timetables were dealt with by HMI alone. Some of the larger LEAs did however issue circulars on the curriculum to schools. In these cases, HMI accepted them and their criticisms were based on the LEA's guidelines. It is known that at least one HMI in 1911 devoted much of his time to the preparation and criticism of timetables and lectured to teachers on the subject. Rough drafts of timetables were sent to him and were then annotated and returned to the headteacher: if they were not considered satisfactory, further discussion would be postponed until the next visit. Apparently in this case the LEA did not concern itself in the negotiations.

Before approval could be given, HMI had to be satisfied on the balance between subjects, the content of lessons and their length. Selby-Bigge admitted that the subject matter of lessons 'is so dependent on the taste and capability of the individual teacher that serious criticism under this head is seldom necessary'. More positively, 'H.M. Inspector may find it profitable to lay stress on subjects which have recently come to the front, or to deprecate others which he feels to be comparatively unimportant' (L.A. Selby-Bigge, Memorandum, 19 May 1911, Public Record Office, hereinafter PRO, Ed 24/229). It may be argued that HMI's task of the close supervision of the timetable and curriculum conflicted with the stated aims of *Suggestions* in acting as a brake on experimentation and innovation. At the NUT Annual Conference at Aberystwyth in 1911, a former President, T.P. Sykes, protested at the minute regulation of the arrangement of work in elementary schools and gave examples of unrealistic suggestions made by HMI which led to confusion in the classroom. Sykes advocated that schemes of work should be drawn up by the staff of a school within the broad lines laid down by the Board and LEA 'because no true teacher ever realises his full task until he comes face to face with the children to be educated. . . . Timetables, schemes of work and notes of lessons cannot be regarded as educational instruments at all' (Sykes, 1911, p. 7). The removal of responsibility for detailed approval of the timetables by HMI was called for. It was not until 1926 that this change was effected.

While working towards an enlightened primary philosophy HMI was caught in the network of tensions between progressivism in elementary schools, which many of them supported, and their role as Inspectors which required them to concentrate on ensuring that standards were maintained in schools. Official publications, however, continued to advocate a liberal approach. The successive editions of *Suggestions* (from 1927, retitled *Handbook of Suggestions*) offered greater freedom to teachers, and in 1912, following a visit by Edmond Holmes to Maria Montessori's schools in Rome, the Board published an account of his impressions in an educational pamphlet, *The Montessori System of Education*.

Much innovation came from other sources. Margaret McMillan, for instance, pioneered the English nursery school early in the century (Whitbread, 1972, p. 61); Edmond Holmes's book, *What Is*

and What Might Be (1911), which attacked the traditional elementary school, inspired educationists eager for change. The New
Education Fellowship, formed in 1914 by Holmes, Percy Nunn,
Michael Sadler and other leading figures, proved to be instru-
mental in formulating a philosophy of elementary education. This
influence can be seen, for example, in the two Hadow Reports on
the Primary School (1931) and the Infant School (1933) (see
Selleck, 1972, p. 143). The anonymity expected of HMI meant
that they were excluded from commenting on current trends.
In John Adams's book *Educational Movements and Methods*
(1924), chapters on co-education, the Dalton Plan, the Montessori
system and eurythmics were written respectively by a secretary of
an education committee, the Chief Inspector of the LCC and two
university educationists. However, HMI did have a part to play
in these changes. As Raymont remarked in his *Modern Education*
(1934):

> [HMI] must, if he be honest, be hard upon laziness, but he
> may now, without failing in his duty, look with a kindly eye
> upon the well-meaning blunderer. He may – and this is one of
> the most valuable of his functions – act as a carrier of
> information about improved methods, for he sees scores of
> schools, whereas the teacher sees only his own (p. 333).

Legislation and the findings of consultative committees also
affected HMIs' work. The 1918 Education Act, which enforced
compulsory attendance at school up to the age of 14, emphasized
the need for LEAs to make changes in the education of children
below the age of 11. This was recognized by the Board in 1925,
when Circular 1350 stated that 11 was the most suitable age for
the ending of the primary school stage. In the following year, the
Code made an important departure from previous practice by
withdrawing all detailed reference to the curriculum. Teachers
no longer had to obtain the Board's approval either on content or
distribution of time between different subjects. The Annual
Report for 1926 announced that detailed comment and advice
would in future be confined to the *Handbook of Suggestions*, a
revised edition of which was then in course of preparation. The
volume appeared in 1927 and contained an interesting Preface. It
reproduced the Introduction to the Code which had been
reprinted each year between 1904 and 1926. Under the heading
The Need for a Broad Conception of the Purpose of the School,
the 1927 edition considered the earlier statement to be no longer
appropriate in regarding 'the teaching of the various subjects and

the other activities of the school in the light of their contribution towards a general purpose, as means, that is, rather than ends' (pp. 8–9). In the words of the 1931 Consultative Committee on the Primary School, 'the curriculum is to be thought of in terms of activity and experience rather than of knowledge to be acquired and facts to be stored' (p. 93). The *Handbook* acknowledged that the Report of the Consultative Committee on *The Education of the Adolescent*, published in 1926, had been an important influence. The Hadow Report (1931) recommended that schooling up to 11 plus should be known by the general name of primary education and that a second stage, secondary, should then follow. Re-organization of elementary education on Hadow lines, making separate provision for the two age groups, proceeded rapidly from 1928.

The implications of these changes for the Inspectorate, both in its mode of working and in its internal organization, were quickly realized. Detailed supervision of the curriculum of primary schools was no longer appropriate, as the earlier Raymont quotation makes clear. The upper levels of the Inspectorate were restructured and unified under a Senior Chief Inspector (see Chapter 9). The freer flow of information within the Inspectorate was facilitated by the appointment of nine Divisional Inspectors who were responsible for co-ordinating the work of HMI at each stage of education as well as organizing divisional inquiries and inspections.

The 1944 Education Act established primary education as the first stage in a continuous system of education. The Ministry of Education, the successor to the Board, recognized that with the disappearance of the elementary school, the *Handbook of Suggestions* was no longer appropriate. It was replaced by a volume entitled *Primary Education*, written by HMI and published in 1959. The contents were based on the observations of HMI in schools in all parts of the country and on discussions with teachers about their work. One of the main features of primary education, it was suggested, was 'the deepening concern with children as children', an attitude which had spread from nursery and infant schools to the junior schools. The stress was on 'needs'. Thus, *Primary Education* drew attention to the importance of an awareness of the child as a whole with interdependent spiritual, emotional, intellectual and physical needs. However, no less significant was the quality of children's learning together with a sense of standards. The cramping effects of the 11 plus examination, the process of allocating children to secondary education, was noted and flexible organization rather than streaming was advocated. For the most part, the contributions of individual HMI to promoting good primary practice tended to pass unrecognized behind the official mask. Between the two world wars, a number of HMI were recruited who were committed to the progressive cause. Robin Tanner, himself a practising and talented artist, was influential in the field of art education. Jennie Mack, who ran a series of short courses for infant heads for many years, generated a national network of heads, training college tutors, inspectors and advisers who put into practice locally the teaching methods, techniques and classroom organization advocated at these courses. Christian Schiller organized similar courses in the junior field (Burrows, 1978, p. 26). More recently, Edith Biggs, as Staff Inspector for mathematics travelled the country with workshops, providing opportunities for teachers to become aware of the 'New Mathematics'.

Plowden and after

The official acceptance by the Ministry of progressive primary education was reflected in a major inquiry into this phase. In 1963, the Central Advisory Council for England under its chairperson, Lady Plowden, was asked 'to consider primary education in all its aspects, and the transition to secondary education'. Some of its important recommendations, published in its Report in 1967, included the designation of educational priority areas to ameliorate the socially disadvantaged, the expansion of nursery education and changes in the age of transfer in primary education with first schools for five to eight year olds, followed by middle schools for eight to twelves. The government adopted many of these recommendations very quickly.

More controversial was what became known as the 'Plowden philosophy' which depicted children in the majority of schools as self-motivated and making progress at a satisfactory rate. For instance, the Report stated that 'Children's own interests direct their attention to many fields of knowledge and the teacher is alert to provide material, books or experience for the development of their ideas' (para. 289). The Committee further declared that 'we have for the most part described English primary education at its best. That in our belief is very good indeed. Only rarely is it very bad' (para. 1234).

HMI made a substantial contribution to the deliberations of the Committee. They were asked by the Committee to undertake a comprehensive survey of the 20,000 primary schools of England and the whole body of HMI responsible for the inspection of primary schools took part. The schools were to be judged by a classificatory scheme of nine categories, ranging from category one, 'a school of outstanding quality' to category nine, 'a local school where children suffer from laziness, indifference, gross incompetence or unkindness on the part of the staff'. In the first category, HMI placed 109 schools, representing 1 per cent of the total primary school population and in category nine, 28 schools (0.1 per cent). The bulk came under category six, 'run of the mill' schools consisting of 6058 schools (28 per cent), followed by category three, 4155 schools or 23 per cent. These findings confirmed the Committee's view on the state of health of English primary schools in the late 1960s.

The euphoria in educational circles which followed the publication of the Plowden Report soon began to be dispelled. In 1969, the first of the *Black Papers* appeared. Written mainly by academics and teachers holding traditional views on educational issues, they deplored the non-competitive ethos of progressive education and the alleged lowering of standards in schools. A more considered appraisal and analysis, however, was contained in *Perspectives on Plowden* (1969), a volume of essays written by members of the London University Institute of Education which examined some of the statements made in the Report. The book's editor, the philosopher Richard Peters, objected to Plowden's suggestion that there was one ideal method of teaching, as contrasted with the old formal teaching and rote learning. Students at colleges of education, he claimed, were being indoctrinated into this constricting ideology. Robert Dearden noted that of the Report's 555 pages, only three and a half were devoted to a discussion of aims; he also pointed out that the Report's emphasis on the value of personal autonomy required some qualification 'because young children cannot be regarded as fully fledged autonomous agents, in relation to whom the teacher can properly be seen as no more than advisory'. Brian Foss found the Report psychologically disappointing: the view that the child 'must be allowed to develop' emphasized the endogenous aspect of the child about which the teacher could do nothing. The permissive attitude of the teacher to educational standards implied in the Report was deplored by the Director of the Institute, Lionel Elvin. He suggested that, for example,

Plowden's notion of teaching the English language was 'well-meant liberalism turning to cultural treason' (p. 100). And referring to the HMI evaluation of primary schools, Basil Bernstein and Brian Davies called their classificatory scheme 'nine intuitive, hazy categories' (p. 72).

There is some evidence that many of these criticisms of Plowden were accepted by HMI involved in primary school inspection, especially on the question of standards. This can be gathered from a survey of fifty-three primary schools, described as 'open plan' in design, by HMI in the school year 1970–1. All the schools visited had easier access between teaching areas than older schools. The object of the survey was to observe the way the spaces and facilities within teaching spaces were related, and to study the real learning and teaching experiences which a more flexible organization offered. The results of the survey, *Open Plan Primary Schools* (DES, 1972) make interesting reading. On the *deployment of teachers* in co-operative or team teaching situations, the survey recommended that the deployment of staff and the grouping of children should be kept as simple as possible. Concentration of teaching resources in one area and increased specialization by one teacher should grow as children's requirements become more sophisticated. *Group work* and *individual assignments* for children both had their disadvantages. HMI found few signs that the new layout of the buildings led to corresponding changes in teaching techniques. Many individual assignments were considered of doubtful value, being mainly repetitive exercises. The Survey remarked that 'There is a continuing need for "class teaching" to start off a major piece of group work, or to round it off, or to convey information quickly and effectively. The newer techniques of class arrangement do not replace the old, they add to them' (*ibid.*, p. 5). The Inspectors found similar patterns of teaching in many schools even where little co-operative teaching was to be seen. Teachers were recommended to undertake more systematic planning and careful checking in such a situation. HMI commented on instances where children were working at less than capacity. One seven-year-old stated, 'There is so much to choose from I don't know what to do.' Two eight-year-old boys took nearly two hours to write out every sixth and seventh number up to ninety-nine. An English lesson was observed during which over a third of the class queued idly, waiting their turn with the teacher.

Some of the concerns expressed by primary Inspectors on standards in the report were raised in an acute form shortly afterwards with the publicity arising out of the teaching, organization and management of a North London primary school, William Tyndale, between July 1973 and the autumn of 1975. The conflict which arose between teachers, parents, managers and the Inner London Education Authority ultimately led to a public inquiry into the affair conducted by Mr Robin Auld, QC. The report, published in 1976, ran to over 300 pages. Amongst other matters, it highlighted the question of the relationship between HMI and LEA inspectorates.

As far back as 1912, an informal verbal agreement had been made between Sir Robert Blair, the Education Officer for the LCC and F.B. Dale, HMI, Chief Inspector, Elementary Schools, which left the routine inspection of elementary schools to the LCC and the sending of general reports to the Board of Education. As one LCC inspector later recalled, 'Our practice in London was to work in harmony with but quite independently of the other Inspectorate' (Christian, 1922, p. 152). By 1938, only fifty-five schools out of 971 had been inspected under this arrangement. In the case of 515 schools, over half the elementary schools in London, the Board had received no reports by LCC inspectors during the preceding ten years. When, towards the end of the Second World War, it seemed probable that elementary education as a category would disappear, the Board considered it necessary to review inspection arrangements in London. At a meeting held on 19 April 1943 between the Board and LCC officials, the 1912 concordat was reconsidered. The Board's team, consisting of Sir Maurice Holmes, Duckworth, the Senior Chief Inspector, and the Chief Inspectors for Elementary and Technical Education, considered the existing situation 'indefensible'. It was necessary to accept that the authority responsible for inspection was central, and not the LEA (Memorandum, PRO Ed 23/667). The 1944 Education Act subsequently empowered the Minister to cause inspection of every educational establishment (i.e. schools and colleges) at intervals as appeared to him to be appropriate.

During the William Tyndale dispute, visits by teams of ILEA inspectors were made, but as the staff of the Junior School was uncooperative, they were not labelled 'full inspections'. The teachers, for their part, appealed to the DES to hold a public inquiry and inspection to investigate the allegations made against them (ILEA, 1976, p. 245). In fact, the DES refused to intervene, HMI made no visits, no public statement was given nor was evidence offered to the Auld Inquiry. Gretton and Jackson (1976, p. 86) claimed that a retired senior Inspector had informed them that the decision not to intervene in the William Tyndale dispute must have been taken at the highest level. This case illustrates the boundary difficulties which may arise between the central and local inspectorates.

In the same year (1976) the Ruskin College speech sparked off further questioning relating to schooling and was followed by the so-called Great Debate. In the background paper for the DES regional conferences held in February and March 1977, *Educating Our Children*, primary schools came under scrutiny.

> It is necessary, in fact, to ask 'what is taught?' not only in relation to subject names, but in more general terms. Does the primary school give its pupils experience and mastery of a sufficiently broad and demanding range of language? Can most of its pupils apply mathematical skills to the problem of ordinary living? (DES, 1977c, p. 4).

To answer questions such as these, HMI had begun a national survey of primary schools in autumn 1975 which was completed by spring 1977. The report, *Primary Education in England. A Survey by HM Inspectors of Schools*, published by the DES in 1978, was an account of the work of seven- , nine- and eleven-year-old children in 542 representative schools. HMI made their assessments in accordance with agreed schedules which were more sophisticated than those used in connection with Plowden. Each teaching group was visited by two Inspectors.

The economic and demographic climate had changed in the decade between the publication of the Plowden Report and the Primary Survey. Resources were scarcer and the fall in the birth rate had led to a reduction in numbers. However, the Survey was mainly concerned with the content of the children's work and their level of performance; the National Foundation for Educational Research administered objective tests in mathematics and reading. The Survey was critical of a number of issues:

1 More able children were not being extended sufficiently in subjects such as mathematics and reading.
2 Teachers needed considerable knowledge of subjects, especially with older pupils; both science and craft suffered from teachers' lack of skill in selecting and utilizing subject matter.
3 Teaching of skills in isolation did not produce the best results.
4 Priorities should be established and the curriculum kept within realistic bounds.

5 Agreement on curriculum between schools in a locality, both primary and secondary, was to be sought. 'National needs' were to be borne in mind.
6 Children in inner-city schools were more likely than others to be underestimated by their teachers and less likely to be given work which extended their capabilities.
7 An important point was the recommendation for more specialist teachers who could also draw up schemes and give guidance to other members of staff.
8 In-service courses for teachers, in areas such as assessing pupils' needs and in developing teaching methods, should be a part of their professional development.

A similar survey for the younger children in the primary range was carried out by HMI in 1978 and 1979. Some 80 first schools, consisting of 33 taking children from five to eight and 47 from five to nine, were scrutinized, with the focus on curriculum and management of the schools. The Report, entitled *Education 5 to 9*, published in 1982, echoed many of the criticisms of the Primary Survey. HMI concluded that nearly all the pupils made satisfactory starts in mathematics and language, but the older and more able children made too little progress. Overemphasis on basic skills limited the time available for extending the range of curriculum activities. On school management, the Report noted that only a half of the schools held regular staff meetings and fewer than a quarter of the heads encouraged teachers to develop special interests and expertise. Besides stating the need for appropriate in-service training, the Report also paid attention to initial training. It recommended that BEd courses should concentrate on work that contributed to students' professional competence in the classroom.

Many of the views expressed in both Surveys were eventually incorporated into an Inspectorate discussion document *The Curriculum from 5 to 16*, issued in 1985. A follow up to the Survey began in 1982 with a four-year rolling programme of 500 inspections. Jim Rose, the Chief Inspector for Primary Education, in an interview emphasized that, though burdensome, full inspections were the life-blood of primary HMI. Rose stated that the 'integrity' of full inspections of primary schools, as opposed to secondary-style part-inspections, must be maintained (*Times Educational Supplement*, 25 October 1985, p. 7).

Rise of the middle school

One other aspect of inspection needs to be considered, that relating to the middle school. In 1958, a Government White Paper, *Secondary Education for All*, stated that between 10 and 20 per cent of primary school children at the age of 11 were wrongly allocated to grammar and secondary modern schools. A new Labour government in 1964, committed to end selection and promote comprehensive schools, passed legislation that same year allowing LEAs to create middle schools straddling the junior and secondary age ranges. DES Circular 10/65 in the following year encouraged their growth, stating 'The establishment of middle schools with age ranges of eight to 12 or nine to 13 has an immediate attraction in the context of secondary reorganisation on comprehensive lines.' The educational and social advantages of the middle school as part of a three-tier system were also praised by the Plowden Report in 1967. By 1970, the DES had approved middle school schemes in forty-nine LEAs which included eight to twelve, nine to thirteen and ten to thirteen schools, though other combinations were allowed later.

Two publications on the middle school, written by 'specialist members of HM Inspectorate' (Burrows, 1978, p. 33), appeared simultaneously in 1970. *Towards the Middle School* identified various approaches to curriculum: staffing, training and management. A final chapter set out some possible problems for those working in middle schools, such as consistency between educational phases, co-operation with parents and connections with the community (Chapter 7, pp. 54–9). *Launching Middle Schools* was an account of preparations and early experiences in Division No. 15 of the West Riding of Yorkshire, one of the first in the field, based on two HMI Surveys in 1968 and 1969. It was recognized that the middle school experiment was still in its early stages but HMI cautiously concluded that 'the omens may be said to be favourable' (*ibid.*, p. 15).

By the early 1980s, the Inspectorate deemed that an appraisal of middle school education was appropriate for several reasons. The re-organization of local government in 1974 led to the disappearance of a number of LEAs as well as the creation of others; many middle schools became part of new administrative areas. Falling rolls and the viability of small middle schools, economic constraints and public concern with educational standards, required an assessment of these schools which were attended by approximately 22 per cent of eleven-year-olds in the English maintained sector.

The Inspectorate decided to make two separate surveys, one for nine to thirteen schools and separately, because of their different characteristics, of eight to twelve and five to twelve schools. The results of the surveys were published as *9 to 13 Middle Schools. An Illustrative Survey* (DES, 1983a), and *Education 8 to 12 in Combined and Middle Schools: An HMI Survey* (DES, 1985a). Both surveys differed in significant respects from the earlier Primary and Secondary Surveys. *Primary Education in England* (DES, 1978) examined aspects of the work of classes. The *9 to 13 Middle Schools* and *Education 8 to 12* Surveys discussed the life and work of entire schools. Whereas *Aspects of Secondary Education in England* (DES, 1979b) provided a detailed examination of language, mathematics, science and personal and social development in the last two years of compulsory schooling, these two Reports assessed the work of the whole age range in a large number of subjects and areas of the curriculum. The aim was to provide a snapshot of activities rather than select particular aspects of schooling.

The *9 to 13 Middle Schools* Survey involved visits by HMI to forty-eight out of the 610 middle schools which existed in January 1983; those chosen represented a variety but not a statistically representative sample of schools (DES, 1983a, p. 132). The visits, made during 1979 and 1980, were carried out by teams of between ten to thirteen Inspectors, who spent the equivalent of a week in each school.

Some of the conclusions provided little comfort for middle schools. Fewer than half of the survey schools reached generally satisfactory standards in the curriculum as a whole and only five out of forty-eight schools achieved good standards. Whilst stressing that many of the problems touched on in the Report were not confined to middle schools, the implications for future policy were mentioned:

> If 9–13 middle schools are to continue to provide a transition from primary to secondary modes, as originally envisaged, and to perform, age for age, as well as primary and secondary schools are expected to perform, given the present and likely trend of falling rolls, they will become increasingly expensive . . . some of the practical difficulties facing 9–13 middle schools have been revealed in this survey and, in the present economic circumstances, carrying the relatively higher cost of middle

schools sharply decreasing in size will have consequences elsewhere in the system (*ibid.*, pp. 130–1).

Similar doubts on the viability of middle schools were expressed eighteen months later in the *Education 8 to 12* (DES, 1985a) Survey. Some forty-nine of the 388 combined schools existing in January 1981 were visited, 16 five to twelve schools and 33 eight to twelve schools. Inspection procedures were similar to those used in the *9–13* Survey, but with some modifications because of the different age ranges. Each inspection team included subject specialists as well as those who had expertise in that phase of education.

The Report, published at a time when secondary school rolls were falling and LEAs were dismantling their middle schools, like the *9–13* Survey, found that only a half of the schools seen were reaching generally satisfactory standards. HMI also commented on inadequate curriculum planning which resulted in the neglect of subjects such as religious education, craft, design and technology and geography (DES, 1985a, p. 72). However, the Survey concluded that external factors continued to be important in making decisions about the rationalization of school provision (*ibid.*, p. 81).

Conclusion

From the beginning of the present century, the development of progressive methods in primary schools was encouraged by a group of sympathetic HMI. Since the publication of the Plowden Report in 1967, the Inspectorate has voiced its reservations on such matters as the balance and organization of the curriculum, standards and the viability of middle and combined schools. The two recent Surveys on middle and combined schools are examples of the adoption of new procedures in inspecting.

Chapter 4

Influence on secondary schools

Establishment of the Secondary Inspectorate

Although HMI were not involved in the inspection of secondary schools until the beginning of the present century, there had been earlier attempts to enforce such a system. For example, the Endowed Schools Bill of 1869 which was concerned with the reform of the endowed schools, stipulated that a Court of Examiners should be established, to which a number of permanent inspectors, paid by the central government, should be appointed. They would make reports on the whole school every two or three years. The cost of examining was to be borne by the school. This part of the Bill met with fierce opposition from many of the public school headmasters, notably Edward Thring at Uppingham. He asked, 'Who are to examine? A large proportion of the masters of endowed schools are men of good degrees, in many cases of very good degrees. Are they to be examined by their equals in merit, their inferiors possibly in age and experience?' (Parkin, 1898, vol. 1, pp. 172–3). During the Bill's passage through the Commons, this section was deleted and no inspections of endowed schools resulted. A Select Committee of the House of Commons on ministerial responsibility for education reported in 1884. Besides recommending the appointment of a Minister of Public Instruction, it proposed that he should have power in the case of all endowed schools, if deemed expedient, to inspect and examine them. From 1888, the Charity Commissioners began to employ barristers to visit secondary schools, who included some judgments on the teaching and curriculum in their reports, though they received no training for the work.

Mention has been made in Chapter 2 of the creation of the

Science and Art Department with its own small Inspectorate. There was a generous expansion of the definition of the term 'technical instruction' following the legislation of 1889 and 1890 to include a very wide range of subjects taught in secondary schools. However, Science and Art Inspectors were restricted to the task of examining the subjects for which grants had been allocated, rather than taking into account the organization and aims of the school as a whole.

In 1898, the Bill for establishing a Board of Education was introduced which would have given the Board power to 'visit, inspect and examine any school'. The Lord President, the Duke of Devonshire, sounded out the opinion of governing bodies and headmasters of public schools on this matter through Michael Sadler, at the Office of Special Inquiries, and was surprised at their reaction (Grier, 1952, p. 66). Devonshire told the House of Lords:

> Most of them, the largest and most important Public Schools of the country included, have, through their headmasters, expressed the opinion that they are so impressed with the public advantage of a general inspection of Secondary Schools by some competent authority, that they would be willing on certain conditions, although they might have little or nothing to gain by it themselves, to come under such a system of inspection (*Hansard*, 4, 1xviii, col. 673, 14 March 1899).

This co-operative spirit arose from the fact that during the course of the passage of the Bill in the Lords, the clause charging only the officers of the new Board with inspection was dropped. In its place, under Section 3(1) of the Act, inspections could also be conducted by the Universities of Oxford, Cambridge, Victoria (Manchester), Birmingham and London, as well as the City and Guilds of London Institute, for technological subjects, manual instruction and domestic economy only. In 1900, five schools were inspected under this new procedure and the number rose to 137 in 1903, but by 1905 it had fallen to five.

Dramatic changes had meanwhile taken place both outside and within the Board which increased the demand for inspection. By far the most important was the 1902 Education Act which empowered the new Local Education Authorities to provide and aid secondary schools from the rates. LEAs also had the duty 'of considering both the needs of individual schools and their organization and co-ordination over the whole area'. The success of the new municipal secondary school was widely acknowledged:

competition for scholarships offered by local authorities stimulated demand (the number rose from about 2,500 places in 1895 to over 23,500 in 1906) and was furthered by the Board's Regulations of 1905 which required boys and girls intended for the teaching profession to receive a sound general education in a secondary school for three or four years. The Secondary School Regulations of 1907, the work of the new Liberal government, required these schools to offer up to 25 per cent of their places free to pupils from public elementary schools.

Within the Board, the appointment of Robert Morant as its Permanent Secretary led to a reorganization of its internal structure which was reflected in the allocation of inspectorial duties (Allen, 1934, pp. 224–5). There were henceforth three main branches – Elementary, Secondary and Technological – and in 1905 members of the Inspectorate were redeployed to form corresponding branches under these headings. This change called for new inspectorial expertise. Inspection of elementary schools had been traditionally the main occupation of HMI. Now, they were called upon to provide advice and information both for the Board and the LEA where they inspected as well as to develop expertise in inspecting the secondary school.

A Chief Inspector for Secondary Education was appointed in 1904, William Charles Fletcher, who was previously Headmaster of the Liverpool Institute, and a mathematician. Fletcher remained as Chief Inspector until his retirement in 1930. Up to the middle of 1904, the Board relied heavily on the services of the former Science and Art Inspectors: six of the eighteen Inspectors became the core of the Secondary Inspectorate. A further six came from the ranks of the Elementary Branch, one of whom was P.A. Barnett, formerly Principal, Borough Road Training College. One method of supplementing the permanent HMI attached to the Branch was the occasional use made of outside experts, a practice inherited from the Science and Art Department. The Board's Annual Report for 1903–4 lists no fewer than thirty such individuals. They included Arthur Sidgwick, brother of Henry Sidgwick and a distinguished don in his own right, G.C. Coulton, the historian, and Foster Watson, the educational historian. A number were women, consisting of retired heads and others who were subject specialists mainly in foreign languages, physical education and domestic economy. But as Leese has noted (1950, p. 262), the employment of occasional Inspectors was apt to make inspection a cumbrous and expensive business. Some became permanent HMI: J.W.

Headlam, for example, was appointed as Staff Inspector in 1904 after serving on an occasional basis. Two other Staff Inspectors were appointed, R.P. Scott and F. Spencer as well as a scientist, F.B. Stead, four years later.

Morant and Fletcher envisaged the Secondary Inspectorate as a distinctive body of men and women of high academic standing with good teaching experience and able to influence the course of the development of secondary education. The majority of those recruited were drawn from public schools. One reason for this may have been in order to gain the confidence of public schools themselves so that State inspection would be acceptable. This policy was successful. Such schools received no grant from the Board and were not thus subject to compulsory inspection. However, from 1907, when the Board's list of secondary schools recognized as efficient was issued, many of them requested inspection. By 1913, sixty-eight of the 101 Headmasters' Conference schools had been inspected by HMI.

The full inspection

An important feature of secondary school inspection was the invention and use of the 'full inspection'. Elementary schools had been visited by HMI since the time of the Revised Code in order to test the work of both teachers and pupils. Secondary schools, with their larger range of subjects and specialist staffs, required a different approach. The full inspection was conducted by a team of inspectors over a period of several days and they carefully looked at the administration, work and life of a school. The Board justified full inspections in its Annual Report for 1922-3 thus:

A Secondary School covers a wide variety of subjects: it may, and often does, carry many of them to an advanced stage; it may include on its staff men of acknowledged eminence in various branches of learning. But the school cannot be judged by a mere review of the subjects taught: it is a living thing: its life, which may have behind it a long historic tradition, extends beyond the classroom and must be grasped as a whole. Periodically, therefore, a comprehensive inspection of the school must be undertaken. The reason why a body of inspectors should undertake such inspection is not so much that the skill of a specialist is needed to inspect specialists, but that

51

collective judgement on all sides of the school life and work is necessary (Board of Education, 1924, p. 37).

The team of inspectors, which differed from inspection to inspection, was headed by the District Secondary Inspector. It would normally consist of between two and six specialists and might draw on relevant Staff Inspectors or colleagues in other branches. The Board's Annual Report for 1922–3 was also careful to mention that

> The inspectors do not make any claim to be either abler or better teachers or schoolmasters than many whom they meet in the course of their work, nor have any such claims ever been preferred on their behalf. So far as that aspect of things is concerned, they are no more than equals among equals.

If this was the intention, the reality was rather different. John Leese, a former HMI, commented on the full inspection, 'It was to the modern secondary teacher as trying an ordeal as the visit of HM Inspector used to be to the elementary teacher of half a century ago. The chief differences were that whereas the latter lasted a day only, the full inspection took a week' (1950, p. 270). Further, a poor inspection report could have serious consequences for a school, or for an individual teacher's career prospects.

In fact, the nature of the full inspection has not changed in any measurable detail since its inception (see *Reporting Inspections*, DES, 1986b), except that it is no longer confined to the secondary sector of education. Schools were requested, prior to the inspection, to send details of their teaching staffs, curricula, syllabuses, timetables and other information. The Chief Inspector was responsible for appointing each team. The Inspector in charge of the team was called the Reporting Inspector (RI) and it was his responsibility to deploy his colleagues in the most effective way. Those who could offer more than one specialism were particularly useful team members. During the course of the inspection and certainly at the end of it, the team would meet together to discuss its findings. The RI, sometimes with colleagues in attendance, then presented the headteacher with a verbal report and subsequently discussed his/her findings with the governing body, who may or may not have invited the headteacher to attend at some stage in the proceedings. There was no obligation on the part of the governing body to inform the teaching staff of the contents, a fact which roused much criticism from the teachers' unions. Some time after the inspection – the length depended often on the size of the undertaking and on the other commitments of the team – the RI would draw up a report which was sent to the governing body and also to the LEA.

The printed report could be published, the only restriction being that the full report, and not simply extracts from it, was reproduced. Some schools, where the report was favourable, were pleased to copy it in their magazines for the enlightenment of parents and pupils, but the practice was not widespread. The reason for this is not difficult to find. It was customary for HMI to avoid naming individual teachers in reports, a tradition which still continues, but as departments were described, any criticisms, if published, might be resented by members of staff.

Inspectors were not subject to any restriction by the Board in the advice which they offered to schools. On the other hand, the Royal Commission on Secondary Education (Bryce Report) in 1895 had deplored the warping of the curriculum by too exclusive attention to science and arts subjects which attracted grants from South Kensington. As a result, it claimed, the literary subjects had been ignored and the main function of the school, to give a broad humanizing education, had been lost sight of. Mischief arose from the conflict between the attempts to educate and train the mind and the attempt to teach something of immediate commercial utility. Even as late as 1903, the Board's Regulations for Secondary Schools awarded a higher rate of grant to those schools devoting most of their time to science than where a traditional grammar school curriculum was offered.

HMI Mr J.W. Headlam, a classicist by training, vigorously denounced this situation in a *Report on the Teaching of Literary Subjects in Some Secondary Schools* issued in 1902. Banks (1955, p. 37) attributes the Board's recasting of the Secondary Regulations in 1904 to Headlam's Report. The Regulations insisted that the curriculum should provide for a well-balanced education: English, geography and history were allocated not less than 4½ hours per week and 'not less than 3½ hours when one foreign language is taken, or less than 6 hours for two'. These requirements were relaxed in 1907 and the Board noted that great improvements had been made subsequently, through teachers, LEAs and by the efforts and personal influence of the Board's Inspectors (Annual Report, 1908–9, p. 41).

There was no *Handbook of Suggestions* for secondary school teachers but, instead, a series of Circulars drawn up by Inspectors was issued with the same purpose in mind, for instance on the teaching of Latin (1907), geometry and graphic algebra (1909) and English (1910). It is clear from a *Memorandum on Language Teaching in State-Aided Secondary Schools*, issued by the Board in 1909, that information gained from full inspections was being collated by HMI in order to form an impression of the state of teaching in various subjects over the country (p. 7). The results of these surveys began to appear in the Board's Annual Reports, such as those for geography, English and science. The 1910–11 Report, for example, contained an extensive section on the teaching of mathematics in secondary schools, drawn up by the Chief Inspector, W.C. Fletcher (pp. 47–58).

The programme of full inspections was carried out with great speed and on a large scale. By 1912, nearly all the secondary schools receiving grants from the Board had been fully inspected at least once and most of them twice. In the seven years from 1905 to 1912, the number of schools inspected was 1,487, an average of about 200 a year. Some of the less efficient schools were inspected at frequent intervals. By 1914, ninety-five schools had received their third inspection and four schools even their fourth. The strain of such an ambitious programme on the Secondary Inspectorate led to a shortened form of full inspection in 1912. Instead of attempting to cover all the activities of a school, HMI confined themselves to selected activities which required special attention. This move was also welcomed by headteachers, who no longer had to prepare elaborate statistics before the visit.

Alternatives to the full inspection

During the First World War, when many Inspectors were employed in other branches of national work, it proved impossible to continue with full inspections. They were discontinued from 1916 apart from exceptional cases. After the war, the Board decided that the accumulated arrears of inspection made necessary a change in policy. From 1922, full inspections took place at intervals of ten instead of five years. The number of secondary schools inspected continued to fall: whereas 327 underwent a full inspection in 1919–20, there were only 173 in 1923–4 (Memo to Inspectors S. No. 545, June 1931). Fletcher, the Chief Inspector for Secondary Education, was also concerned to find a suitable way of keeping in touch with schools during the long periods between full inspections.

Some solution to the problem was becoming imperative by

1930. The number of grant and efficient schools was steadily growing without any corresponding increase in the Inspectorate; at the same time LEAs were requesting more frequent reports on schools. In order to economize effort and to use limited resources to the best advantage, four alternatives to the full inspection were tried:

i   The *following up procedure* was a visit to the school following a full inspection but after an interval of time.

ii *Supplementary inspections*, advisory visits with no report in view, were popular for a time. A termly programme of supplementary inspections was drawn up by the Office and sent to district inspectors. There were eighty-three in 1925–6, but they had dwindled to sixteen by 1932–3 and fell out of use (Memorandum to Inspectors. No. 574, 31 January 1934).

iii *Interim inspections*, conducted by two Inspectors, involved a report but had limited objectives, e.g. sixth form work in one or more subjects. Besides filling the gap between full inspections, this practice had the advantage of being able to concentrate in depth on an aspect of a school. Inspectors needed to know their schools well in order to carry out interim inspections.

iv *Shortened inspections* were full inspections with reduced panels operating in an area where there was some common problem or sufficient similarity between schools. At Birmingham in 1930, for example, a general survey of curriculum was carried out in a group of schools with less emphasis on specialists' views on particular subjects. The majority of the time was occupied in interviewing headteachers and heads of department rather than in observing lessons.

A fifth alternative, the *area inspection* was put forward at a conference of Secondary Inspectors in 1934. Two HMIs would form the core of the inspection panel for an area such as Westmorland and call for help from colleagues from time to time. As HMI had too little time for routine visits, and with full inspections occurring only every ten years, there was a danger that LEAs might appoint their own inspectors to fill the gap. The area inspection might provide the answer to this threat (Memorandum to Inspectors S. No. 585, 10 October 1934). However, this form of inspection was rarely undertaken.

The need for flexibility in approach to inspection was confined to the Secondary Inspectorate. Full inspections were expensive in man hours. In a school of 300 pupils, four HMI were required for four days, not including visits by specialist colleagues. Cases were cited such as that of a small mixed school which required three panel members and specialists for art, music, boys' and girls' physical education, domestic science and metalwork instruction – nine Inspectors for 150 pupils. The hope expressed by the Chief Inspector of Secondary Schools in 1937, of reducing the interval between full inspections to eight years, was not realized (Memorandum to Inspectors S. No. 600, 13 July 1977).

One interesting facet of a full inspection was the motive for mounting the exercise in the first instance. An Instruction to Inspectors, J.117, stated that teachers were not to be named and that the object was to inspect subjects and not teachers. If an LEA or governing body asked for a named teacher to be inspected, the Inspector was to say that this was not permissible. Headteachers were permitted to show teachers that part of the report which referred to them, but this was not obligatory. The distinction between school inspection and teacher appraisal is still very important today. HMI have been careful not to volunteer to undertake the latter task.

Inter-war years

From the time of the 1907 Secondary School Regulations, the detailed control of the secondary school curriculum was relaxed. The secondary schools now served two groups of pupils, those who would progress to further study and those who would immediately enter an occupation. The Board continued to encourage alternative courses of instruction. After the issue of Circular 1294 by the Board in 1922 which stated that 'it has become necessary for schools in planning their time-tables to exercise a greater freedom than has hitherto been customary', HMI were asked to report how far the schools had availed themselves of this freedom. It seems clear from the responses two years later that no major change had resulted from the Circular. Some of the reasons suggested by HMI included 'Circulars are not read, or if read are put away and forgotten', 'The demand for more freedom is noisy rather than real', 'Distrust of the Board' and 'Girls don't like dropping subjects'. Fletcher added his own opinion on the matter. He deprecated any revolutionary change and would resist demands for change made outside the school. The examinations were a stumbling block and must conform to changes in curricula. Summing up, he wrote, 'I do not think any present action necessary, not even a Committee on the Curriculum. I would rather see the schools go on working quietly as on the whole they are doing and gradually evolving. A Committee would be a sounding board for all the enthusiasts!' (Memorandum to Inspectors S. No. 454, 21 July 1924).

The records of the annual conference of Secondary Inspectors in the inter-war years present a full picture of the issues which were of current concern. HMI played a major role in the administration of the School Certificate Examination which was introduced in 1917. The Examination was taken by pupils who had attended a secondary school for five years; a Higher School Certificate Examination could be taken after a further two years of study. It is significant that when an investigation of the examinations was held in 1931, the panel of twenty-two persons under the Chairman, Cyril Norwood, consisted of thirteen teachers or persons connected with secondary education and as many as nine secondary HMIs (Banks, 1955, p. 89). By 1938, panels of investigators who scrutinized standards in the Higher School Certificate Examination were being drawn up with care to avoid complaint of undue domination by Inspectors.

The popularity of the School Certificate Examination gave rise to an allied issue, homework. On 11 June 1934, a remarkably frank memorandum headed 'Homework: its Place in the Schools', written by E.G. Savage, the Senior Chief Inspector, was issued to the Office and the Inspectorate. It began

> There is perhaps no educational question in which the public are generally more interested than that of Homework, and there is also perhaps no subject upon which we have collectively so little definite information. It is my own experience that neither Headmasters nor teachers can give a reliable statement on this matter. (Memorandum to Inspectors General No. 27)

As homework was officially discouraged in elementary schools, the task of collecting data fell on the shoulders of Secondary School Inspectors. Tabulated returns were required from HMI on the frequency, quantity and duration of homework which was set in their schools; answers to these questions were to be obtained from the children themselves. Expounding his views on the subject at the 1934 Secondary Inspectors Conference, Savage said

57

that the question of giving marks for homework ('a vicious practice') should be added to the Memorandum.

The publication of the HMI survey took the form of a Board of Education Pamphlet, No. 111, and was simply entitled *Homework*. The findings caused a stir, in the press and in Parliament, and some of the larger LEAs adopted the Pamphlet's recommendations for future policy (Gordon, 1980, p. 40). In autumn 1938, a follow-up survey, based on notes of homework in recent full inspection reports, was undertaken, but the outbreak of war put an end to further action on the matter.

Apart from discussions on problems connected with full inspections, the most prominent item on the agenda of secondary conferences was the working of the free place system, popularly known as the '11 plus' examination, and its effects on schooling. Since 1907 when the Free Place Regulations were introduced, candidates were required to attend a public elementary school for at least two years and were expected to pass an attainment test before entering on a secondary school course. The Departmental Committee on Scholarships and Free Places reported in 1920 and made a number of far-reaching recommendations on ways in which selection arrangements could be improved. It suggested that LEAs should take over responsibility from individual schools for administering the entrance examination. In order to test capacity and promise, psychological tests were permitted as a possible alternative to examination of attainment.

Group tests were developed with enthusiasm by Cyril Burt in London from 1917 and Godfrey Thomson in Northumberland from 1921 and later at Moray House, Edinburgh. The Secondary Inspectorate reported on the national use of entrance tests in 1921 and 1922 and were practically unanimous in stating that the standard for free places was distinctly higher than for fee payers (E.H. Pelham to L.A. Selby-Bigge, 16 January 1922, PRO Ed 24/1644). As a result, the 1922 Regulations stipulated that the minimum standard of qualifications should be the same for both groups; it also sanctioned the use of intelligence tests as a supplement to written ones. Fletcher ordered a national survey of LEA procedures which was completed by the summer of 1924 and issued as a Memorandum to Inspectors S. No. 455, 19 August, 1924.

Differences in procedures and testing between LEAs was constantly mentioned in reports of the Secondary Inspectorate. The psychological component was not dominant: by 1928, four-fifths of LEAs confined the written examination to English and arithmetic. In one English paper set by an LEA, use was made of the essay. Fletcher called such a test 'obnoxious' and was 'simply inadmissible' as a test for young children. To provide matter-of-fact subjects under examination conditions was very difficult, and would lead children to 'either rebel or write rubbish, or take refuge in insincerity' (Memorandum, 19 August 1924, PRO Ed 22/128).

A pamphlet produced by the Inspectorate in the Board of Education series entitled *Free Place Examinations* (1928) expressed some of their doubts about procedures, particularly on the use of intelligence tests. It stated that 'A general use of these tests in making awards would be premature' (p. 55). However, by 1936, a Supplement to the 1928 pamphlet advised that the intelligence test and each of the attainment tests should be assigned equal weight. In the following year, the *Handbook of Suggestions* for the first time acknowledged the notion of 'mental age', created by psychological testing, as the basis of classification of pupils in primary schools rather than formal attainment or chronological age. It suggested that pupils should be arranged in at least two 'streams', A and B, with the brighter forming the potential 'Junior Scholarship' class (Board of Education, 1937, pp. 31-2).

The investigation of the workings of the examination took up an increasing amount of Secondary Inspectors' time up to 1939. At the 1934 Secondary Conference, there were no fewer than 250 points which came up for discussion on free places, including age allowance, weighting of subjects, age of entry, the prognostic value of a single test, the possibility of assessing temperament, school records, the effects of special coaching, the elimination of subjective judgment in the examiner and the meaning of 'fitness for secondary education'.

HMI involvement in the organization and administration of the examinations varied. Some LEAs co-opted Inspectors on to their examining Council, though this was officially discouraged (Memorandum to Inspectors S. No. 600, 14 July 1937). 'Semi-official' help, however, might be given, including examining, though this had to be carried out in the Inspector's free time. In every LEA, there was close monitoring by HMI. Mr A.F. Watts tried out an experiment in Willesden, Middlesex, where the pressure on secondary school places was very heavy. With the object of testing the effects of coaching for the examination, Watts took two eleven-year-old groups of similar abilities, coaching one group for twelve weeks in English, arithmetic and intelligence tests. When the tests were repeated at the end of this period, the coached group achieved vastly superior scores (Report of Malvern Conference, 18–20 July 1938).

'Secondary education for all'

This increase in the duties of the Secondary Inspectorate between the two world wars was acknowledged by the Norwood Committee on Curriculum and Examinations which reported in 1943. There had been a rapid growth in the number of secondary schools during this time whilst recruitment of HMI had been negligible. The burden of administrative work placed on Inspectors' shoulders had also increased. One consequence was that full inspections of schools had become in the words of the Committee 'less frequent and more hurried' (Board of Education, 1943, p. 50). It was recommended that the number of HMI should be augmented to enable a full inspection of each school every five years and to maintain real contact in the intervening years.

The heavy backlog of reporting brought about by the Second World War became a priority for the Inspectorate in the 1950s. The 1944 Education Act, which provided for separate primary, secondary and further stages of education and the raising of the school leaving age to fifteen, presented many problems for the Minister and the new Ministry of Education which required the expertise of HMI. A massive recruitment of new Inspectors – from 361 in 1946 to 513 by 1948 – was accompanied by the abolition of the distinction between Elementary and Secondary Inspectors.

The provision of 'secondary education for all' followed the lines of the recommendations of the Spens Report on Secondary Education (1938), that there should be three kinds of secondary school – grammar, modern and technical. In practice, the secondary technical school failed to develop on a national basis. A bipartite system was the more usual pattern, consisting of grammar schools and secondary modern schools, the latter taking approximately 70 per cent of the school population. Although parity of esteem between the two types of secondary schools was officially encouraged (see Taylor, 1963, pp. 95 ff), the secondary modern school, which aimed to develop the interests of the children rather than focus on traditional school subjects, failed to convince parents as well as employers of its worth.

Details of the advice given to the Ministry by HMI on this issue are not known. However, in 1958, Geoffrey Lloyd, then

Minister, in a White Paper *Secondary Education for All: A New Drive*, urged LEAs to provide greater opportunities for secondary moderns. Edward Boyle, Parliamentary Secretary to the Ministry at the time, later wrote

> The 1958 policy came too late; the only possible means of preserving a bipartite system would have been the encouragement of GCE courses in all secondary modern schools *from the first*; and that is what some senior officials at the Ministry had wanted to do, but unfortunately they found themselves opposed (most unwisely) by Her Majesty's Inspectors (Boyle quoted in Gosden, 1983, p. 32).

Educational initiatives in the East Riding of Yorkshire non-selective schools had also been discouraged by members of the Inspectorate. They forecast that 'the attempt to provide a variety of courses for children of different abilities within one school was foredoomed to failure' (Quoted in Elton, 1974, p. 24).

By the 1960s, the topic of comprehensive schools became central to discussions on the nature of secondary education. The Labour Party Manifesto for the 1964 General Election promised to end social and educational segregation by introducing comprehensive schools. Crosland was appointed Minister in January 1965 and by July, Circular 10/65, describing the six forms of comprehensive organization which LEAs might adopt, was issued. Crosland was asked five years later by Maurice Kogan, 'Could you say how you arrived, or why you arrived, at six optional schemes? Was this you, or the HMIs, or who?' Crosland confirmed that the details of the options were mainly a product of thinking in the Inspectorate (Kogan, 1971, p. 188). HMI were subsequently involved in scrutinizing schemes for comprehensive education submitted by LEAs and advising Ministers on the soundness or otherwise of the plans. They were also involved in discussions with LEAs and with deputations received by the Minister at Curzon Street and later at Elizabeth House.

After the backlog of full inspections had been adequately dealt with in the period 1955–60, this aspect of HMIs' work diminished. Much energy was expended on comprehensive reorganization but there were other new demands. A third year for training non-graduate teachers was added in 1960 and discussions on the content of the courses involved both phase and subject Inspectors. The Schools Council for Curriculum and Examinations, established in 1964, also occupied the time of many HMI who served in the capacity of assessor or on a seconded basis to the

Council. The period between the 1960s and the early 1970s may be characterized for the Secondary Inspectorate as one of uncertainty. The 1968 Select Committee pointed out that the number of full inspections had diminished, and that much of their work was now shared by the local inspectorates and, through the Schools Council, by the teachers themselves. HMI played an active part in connection with the Central Advisory Council's consideration of education of children of average or below average ability between the ages of thirteen and sixteen. The Council's findings, the Newsom Report, was written by two HMI, David Ayerst, an assessor and Peggy Marshall, the Secretary (Kogan and Packwood, 1974, p. 27).

The Secondary Inspectorate and the curriculum

From the early 1970s the Inspectorate began to resuscitate an interest in the curriculum, taking up the role they formerly played in devising the *Handbook of Suggestions*. Internal discussions on the nature of subjects and their contributions to the curriculum anticipated the Great Debate launched in October 1976. A group of HMI was convened in April 1975 to consider the nature and purpose of the curriculum. By September 1976, the group had drafted a series of papers which were contributed to a DES Conference on 'The Secondary Curriculum', held at Oxford University. These discussions enabled the Secondary Inspectorate to move with some speed when some public response was vital. The DES concluded in the Green Paper *Education in Schools. A Consultative Document* published in July 1977, 'that the time has come to try to establish generally accepted principles for the composition of the secondary curriculum for all pupils' (DES, 1977a, p. 11). This statement echoed the view expressed in the Yellow Book of the previous year, when the curriculum for comprehensive schools was scrutinized, and a 'protected' or core element of a common curriculum was advocated.

HMI response was fairly swift. In December 1977, *Curriculum 11 to 16*, a series of working papers by the Inspectorate and known as 'The Red Book' was published. The Foreword stated that 'These papers have been overtaken by events', but were nevertheless an important contribution to the debate (no parallel document was issued for the primary curriculum). In place of a 'protected core', the Inspectorate argued for a common curriculum which was concerned with introducing certain essential areas of experience to pupils. A checklist of these experiences – aesthetic and creative, ethical, linguistic, mathematical, physical, scientific, social and political, and spiritual – was advocated by HMI as the basis for curriculum construction.

Differences in approach to the curriculum between DES and HMI were apparent in the papers issued by the two bodies. The brief DES consultative document *A Framework for the School Curriculum* in January 1980 made an attempt to stipulate the core curriculum – English, mathematics, modern language, religious education, physical education and preparation for adult and working life: for the first three subjects the percentage of the total time available to be spent on each subject was laid down. This was shortly followed by *A View of the Curriculum* written by HMI, in response to a DES invitation. Once more the 'areas of experience' approach was suggested (DES, 1981a, p. 3). In March 1981, the DES issued a paper *The School Curriculum* which took into account the two HMI discussion documents as well as its own *Framework* statement. Wide ranging consultations had taken place since the publication of these three papers and it seems that HMI thinking had influenced the more moderate approach to the secondary curriculum which it now advocated. How much discussion had taken place between HMI and DES before the issue of *The School Curriculum* is not known. However, the fact that the parallel statements, though differing in emphasis, could be issued on the curriculum illustrates the independence of HMI judgment, uninfluenced by the Department, on professional matters.

HMI observations on the school curriculum were based on a national survey of pupils in their fourth and fifth years of secondary education undertaken during the years 1975–8. A 10 per cent sample was used. The survey, entitled *Aspects of Secondary Education*, pointed out that the traditional nature of the secondary curriculum defined by subject specialisms reinforces this habit of operating in isolation (p. 284). It recommended that schools should develop a more explicit rationale of the curriculum as a whole. It was particularly necessary for schools to have some criteria whereby they could assess their curricular provision and resources, especially at a time of falling rolls and economic cutbacks. Evidence given before the Education, Science and Arts Committee of the House of Commons on the Secondary School Curriculum and Examinations in 1981 by HMI confirmed their advocacy of curriculum-led staffing and the development of self-evaluation techniques in schools (Report, vol. II, 1982, Q. 484).

The Inspectorate did not confine their activities to making statements on the curriculum. In November 1977, the DES issued Circular 14/77 to LEAs requesting replies on six main areas: local arrangements for co-ordination and development; curricular balance and breadth; select subject areas; transition between schools; school records; and preparation for working life. The result of the review appeared in *Local Authority Arrangements for the School Curriculum* in 1979. The Department promised to issue a Circular on curricular policy. Before this, following the Oxford Conference of September 1976, a decision was made to establish an exercise on curricular inquiry, with schools joining LEA advisers and HMI in reviewing their own curricula. Five LEAs – Cheshire, Hampshire, Lancashire, Nottinghamshire and Wigan – participated in the experiment, based on forty-one secondary schools.

From January 1977 until December 1982, a unique pattern of working was established between schools, LEA advisers and HMI. The group set itself two tasks:

1 schools were to evaluate their own provision, in areas such as curricular policy and departmental aims and objects with an emphasis on improving the quality of learning;
2 deliberations of (1) would lead to the construction, analysis and testing of curricular patterns.

HMI and LEA advisers spent much of their time in schools, with teachers also able to make visits within their own LEA. Writing groups were formed and monitoring documents were analysed. A second Red Book, *Curriculum 11 to 16: A Review of Progress* appeared in May 1981. The last year of the enquiry, 1982, was occupied with schools restating their views of the entitlement curriculum and LEAs producing overall statements: the partnership in each LEA then prepared its final publication. The exercise and findings were described in a document prepared by HMI, *Curriculum 11 to 16. Towards a Statement of Entitlement* (DES, 1983f). Such collaboration between HMI and LEA advisory services had been commended in the Rayner Report: 'These contacts provide a further invaluable source through which HM Inspectorate can help to stimulate local thinking, to spread the impact of their national findings based on inspection and to encourage local action and development' (DES, 1982a, para. 3.43).

Following the publication of all HMI reports of full inspections of schools from January 1983, a series of small pamphlets has been issued by the DES entitled *Education Observed* which review aspects of education arising from the reporting. The second in the series summarized HMI finds from the twenty-seven 11–16 comprehensive schools reports published between January 1983 and May 1984 (seventeen of these reports followed 'short inspections'). HMI commented on a number of short-comings: there was a need to improve liaison between feeder schools; teachers did not have sufficiently high expectations of their pupils; lessons were 'teacher dominated'; the curriculum for the less able in fourth and fifth years lacked breadth and balance; and teachers were encouraged to examine how their subject contributed to the curriculum as a whole (DES, 1984b, p. 12).

Conclusion

The inspection of secondary schools did not begin until much later than that of elementary schools. The Secondary Inspectorate, created in 1904, was responsible for devising the full inspection as a way of inspecting a range of subjects. This procedure was eventually applied to all sections of education and is still widely used today. Since 1976, many of the curriculum documents emanating from the Inspectorate have stated the case for a coherent common curriculum for the eleven to sixteen age range and the notion of an entitlement curriculum.

Chapter 5

Influence on further, higher and teacher education

In Chapter 1 we suggested that one of the two major strands in the history of the Inspectorate was the technical branch which developed out of the Science and Arts Department/South Kensington tradition. This was to have a powerful influence on further education, and it has often been considered that the control exerted by HMI on further education has tended to be much firmer than the influence over schools. This FE influence developed into an HMI concern for higher education arising out of the growth of higher education work in technical colleges and polytechnics (for example, the external degrees of the University of London); after 1965 this was given a further impetus when the binary policy was officially accepted in Crosland's Woolwich speech. One of the less fortunate distinctions between universities and polytechnics is the fact that HE work in polytechnics is inspected by HMI, who have no right of entry to universities (except to extra-mural studies and courses for initial teacher training).

HMI have had a strong interest in teacher education since 1842. One of the landmarks in the educational history of any country is the point at which teacher education ceases to be regarded as part of secondary education and is absorbed into the higher education system; as we shall see, this link with teacher training provided HMI with another very important point of entry into higher education, including eventually the university departments of education.

We outlined in Chapter 1 the development of Inspectors for Science and Art who although not technically part of HMI until 1901 were in other respects, a powerful strand in the Inspectorate tradition. Further education was typically unplanned and uncoordinated in any national or even regional way. Individual initiatives were taken; some of them developed and survived, some remained in existence in very different forms, whilst others disappeared from the scene.

Donnelly and the South Kensington Inspectors

We saw in Chapter 1 that Donnelly was the crucial figure in introducing science into schools from 1859 to 1899, the whole of his period at the Science and Art Department. Donnelly was also important in some post-school developments, but not to the same extent. Although the Science and Art Department was reponsible for much more than paying the grant to schools, there was nothing in the further education world to parallel the elementary school system even in the incomplete state that existed before and after the 1870 Act. Nevertheless, Donnelly and other Science and Art Inspectors managed to carry through a number of improvements. For example, after the 1867 Paris Exhibition, it was acknowledged that British manufacturers had been outclassed and that an important factor was the absence of adequate technical instruction in Great Britain. A Select Committee was set up, and Donnelly appeared before it. Donnelly was in favour of a central College of Science which would train teachers and attract some students away from academic subjects in universities. But not until 1888 did Donnelly's idea become a reality in the form of the Royal College of Science. Meanwhile, there had been other national attempts to deal with the problem: a Royal Commission on Scientific Instruction and the Advancement of Science (1875) chaired by the Duke of Devonshire, for example, considered the Donnelly proposal, but less expensive 'solutions' were preferred by the Treasury.

Most of Donnelly's achievements in further education were unfortunately local and opportunistic rather than national: in 1877 he advised the Clothmakers' Company on the need for a central technical training institution, and this later resulted in the City and Guilds Industrial University; similarly, the Drapers' Company were persuaded to establish a school of woodcarving, also in South Kensington.

Donnelly can also be credited with influencing the Samuelson Commission on Technical Education (1881–4) which was concerned with the dearth of technical education as well as its unregulated, haphazard growth. But Donnelly's ambitions were hampered by the unwillingness of government to spend public money and the unwillingness of employers to spend any of theirs on technical education or training. On the debit side, however, Donnelly must be criticized, in retrospect, for wishing to keep his South Kensington empire separate from the rest of the emerging education system; his successes were thus almost inevitably 'patchy' if seen from a national point of view (Armytage, 1950, p. 19).

In 1880 the Livery Companies founded the City and Guilds of London Institute for the advancement of technical education. One of the major activities of the Institute was the promotion of a system of evening classes leading to City and Guilds examinations. The Institute also founded the Finsbury Technical College which was regarded as a model college catering for both evening and day students. The South Kensington Inspectors were interested in these developments, but they were not greatly involved: the initiative had come from private endowments rather than from the central authority in education. Similarly, in 1880 Quintin Hogg established the Regent Street Polytechnic, a college which was to have a long and distinguished part to play in the history of further and higher education, but this too was a private initiative not, in origin, part of national educational policy. After 1889 the London Technical Education Board took over responsibility for the polytechnics, and some national funding was involved.

Musgrave has suggested another deep-rooted problem that the Science and Art Inspectors had to contend with – secrecy.

In 1872 the Royal Society of Arts founded the first strictly technological examinations. Students did not come forward due to fear by employers of losing trade secrets. For the same reason when . . . Donnelly . . . travelled through the North to aid this scheme, manufacturers said that they would do all possible to stop it. Opposition to the creation of the City and Guilds was expressed on similar grounds. . . . One of the reasons given for lack of support to Sheffield Technical College was fear of losing trade secrets. In the early nineties Professor Arnold, the metallurgist of Sheffield University, was allowed to visit all local works, but as part of his conditions of service, was under an interdict that he would not write a textbook. In this case it was not only that the manufacturers of Sheffield did not want their English rivals to know their processes, but they were also afraid of imitation by the Germans and Americans (Musgrave, 1970, p. 155).

It was not just in Sheffield nor in the steel industry alone that secrecy was a hindrance. The Senior Science and Art Inspector in the North West Division wrote in 1895 'In some instances manufacturers are perfectly antagonistic, as they say they are afraid of trade secrets being revealed.' In 1901, the Senior HMI for the Northern Division wrote of the lack of demand for the trained man, 'he might, if employed, become familiar with the trade processes peculiar to his employers and, having improved upon them, might sell his information to rival firms in the neighbourhood' (*ibid.*).

According to Leese (1950, p. 309) the key-note of educational history from 1890 to 1900 was the systematizing of elementary, secondary and technical education. Leese suggests that such was the confusion at the end of the century that the greatest need was to create an efficient technical Inspectorate who could make a national survey of the field.

In 1901 the South Kensington Inspectors were by Order in Council made HMI. In 1904, Mr C.A. Buckmaster became Chief Inspector of the Technological Branch and divided the country into five Divisions. Hitherto Inspectors had looked at individual institutions, but had not considered the technical education provision in whole areas. After 1902, when it became the duty of each local authority to make provision on an area basis, Inspectors began to produce general and area reports. Morant also asked the Chief Inspector and the four senior Technical Inspectors to write down their views on the organization of technical education. In 1908 the very energetic and talented F. Pullinger was promoted to Chief Inspector and initiated a programme of national systematization, following a survey he carried out (Sherington, 1981, p. 13). Detailed report forms provided information for each area annually. Reports were sent to each local authority, thus providing a basis for local planning as well as 'intelligence' information for the central authority. Two major defects were identified: first, the lack of students able to take advantage of instruction in technical institutions; second, the lack of co-ordination between the various courses and examinations.

Before 1902 evening schools were of three very different kinds: continuation elementary schools; Science and Art schools; and Technological Institutes supervised by the City and Guilds. From 1902 to 1908 these were brought together locally and nationally – locally by the local authority, nationally by the Board of Education. There was also by now one system of inspection.

Another major defect related to the course system: prior to the Pullinger rationalization, classes and certificates were rarely linked together in any coherent programme. Pullinger and his HMI, supported by some local authorities and examining bodies, began to implement a policy of sequential programmes with built-in prerequisites. After 1908, grouped courses tended to be planned in three levels: elementary, higher and advanced. The Board of Education endorsed local authority certificates and provided grants for them. A pamphlet on this Course Certificate system was written by an HMI and issued by the Board in 1909.

National Certificates

In 1911 another stage of rationalization took place when the grouped course system was replaced by a new 'National' Certificate. After some initial differences of opinion with the City and Guilds Institute a good deal of progress was made. Pullinger died in 1921, but his place was taken by A. Abbott who persisted with the same policy. The City and Guilds Institute was encouraged to expand its advisory committees to make them more widely representative. 'HMI sat on all advisory committees, and exercised very great influence' (Leese, 1950, p. 313). In 1923 another example of progress through examinations took place: the Board of Education and the Inspectors co-operated with the Institute of Mechanical Engineers to establish National Certificate courses. The aim was to have nationally accepted qualifications which involved practical and theoretical studies. This was a successful initiative which survived the war years and eventually was incorporated into the post-war system. Inspectors were involved in the supervision and approval of courses; the examinations also had to be open to HMI who had the right of access to all written work produced throughout the course and to the examinations. Similar co-operation took place with the Royal Institute of Chemistry, the Institution of Electrical Engineers, the Institute of Builders, the Institute of Naval Architects, and the Company of Shipwrights. In each case a joint committee was established, and the Board of Education's representative was always an HMI with the necessary technical knowledge.

HMI tended to become more powerful as a result of these National Certificate arrangements: when an institution applied for recognition under one of the schemes, an HMI would inspect in order to report on the adequacy of the resources (including the teachers) as well as the syllabus; at the end of the examining process copies of assessors' reports would be sent to HMI who would enquire into any criticisms. Leese (1950, p. 316) also notes that it was not easy to recruit sufficient technical HMI with the appropriate qualifications and experience; nevertheless, numbers grew steadily.

Two levels of National Certificate evolved; the Ordinary Certificate after three years' part-time study, and the Higher Certificate after two more years of part-time study. Equivalent diploma courses were available on a full-time basis, but student numbers were low. This was the major shortcoming of the new course arrangements: the part-time structure inevitably meant high rates of drop-out and failure. The Malcolm Committee (1928), which was set up by Lord Eustace Percy (President of the Board of Education, 1925–9) recommended a greater emphasis on full-time courses as well as the expansion of part-time day courses, but employers were reluctant to get involved in the expense of day release schemes. The Malcolm Report also recommended that the Board should negotiate with representative bodies in each industry and with local authorities for three purposes: first, to inform trade and industry about the educational system; second, to help trade and industry to formulate their views; and finally, to consider how these views could be met. In the same year (1928), Lord Eustace Percy set up a Committee on Education for Salesmanship, chaired by Sir F. Goodenough. Two HMI acted as assessors, and the committee also relied heavily on other HMI who had made studies of European practices in this field. Another important comparative study carried out by HMI was on *Trades Schools on the Continent* (1932) by the Chief Inspector, A. Abbott and Staff Inspector, J.E. Dalton. This report painted an all too familiar picture of lack of interest in training in England compared with European rivals. The other major contrast was that European countries appeared to have a much stronger national planning machinery, whereas in England planning was, if it existed at all, only regional. In 1937 the Board, with the help of HMI, produced a report on *Co-operation in Technical Education* which promised £12 million nationally, as well as encouraging local authorities to take initiatives. But the Second World War had started before the report could be implemented.

Further education post-1944

Before the 1944 Education Act there was no system of further education. There were areas of interest and activity, but in general much ignorance and apathy which HMI could not overcome. With a few notable exceptions, such as Selby-Bigge and Lord Eustace Percy, there was little support within the Board of Education for the Technical Inspectorate. After 1944, however, a system began to emerge. The 1944 Act separated education into three stages: primary, secondary and further. All LEAs were given responsibility for further education and were required to submit schemes to the Ministry of Education. In some respects, HMI acted as the intermediaries, being consulted both by LEAs and by officials at the Ministry. In 1945 the Percy Report recommended a number of innovations including the development of ten Regional Advisory Councils (RACs) to cover the whole of England and Wales, co-ordinating the provision of courses within each region. This developed into the system whereby an HMI in each region was appointed as the Regional Staff Inspector (RSI) with the responsibility of approving every course in further education. The ten RACs were co-ordinated on a national scale by a National Council of Technology which had responsibility for giving advice to the Ministry. There was also a National Academic Board to co-ordinate examinations and awards. HMI were involved in both. In the following year (1946) the Report of the Barlow Committee was published. The committee recommended that industrial growth would demand much more highly trained scientific and technical manpower. The committee was more concerned with university provision, however, than further education.

During the period 1956–1972 there was some further expansion. In 1956 the White Paper *Technical Education* set out a five year programme which proposed the designation of ten Colleges of Advanced Technology concentrating on higher level courses, including the new Diploma in Technology. In 1957 the Jackson Report on *The Supply and Training of Teachers for Technical Colleges* made recommendations to cope with the increasing demand for suitably qualified staff. In 1959 the Crowther Report criticized the existing provision for the fifteen–eighteen age group and the over-reliance on part-time evening courses with high rates of drop-out and failure. The waste of talent among able young people was the dominant theme of this report. This was followed in 1961 by a White Paper *Better Opportunities in Technical Education*. Again the over-reliance on evening courses was criticized and the need for an expansion of full-time courses and sandwich courses was recommended as a matter of urgency. Much of this had a very familiar ring to HMI who had made similar proposals before the war.

In 1963 the Robbins Report made further recommendations for technical courses in higher education. More degree level work was needed and to cope with the validation of such degree courses a new Council for National Academic Awards (CNAA) was established by Royal Charter (1964). All this work was closely scrutinized by HMI. The 1966 White Paper *A Plan for Polytechnics and Other Colleges* did not accept the whole of the Robbins recommendations for an integrated expansion of higher education; instead a binary system was advocated. Whilst both the university sector and the local authority sector of higher education would be increased, the polytechnics and other local authority colleges were planned to expand faster and to a greater extent. The fact that this so-called public sector would eventually amount to more than 50 per cent of higher education was not insignificant as far as HMI were concerned: as the HMI writ did not run within the university sector, if they wanted to control higher education then it was important to expand the public sector.

Vocationalism

Since 1973 there has been another important development, namely the switch of emphasis and funding away from education to training – away from the DES to the Department of Employment's Manpower Services Commission (MSC). This was signalled to some extent by the 1964 Industrial Training Act, but even more important was the 1973 Employment and Training Act which paved the way for the establishment of the MSC in January 1974. Since then it would be no exaggeration to say that most of the innovation and development has come from the MSC; in 1976 the publication *Towards a Comprehensive Manpower Policy* and in 1977 *Young People and Work* outlined very broadly the plans for the future. In 1979 the Youth Opportunities Programme (YOP) was started, extended in the following year to a programme for 'unified vocational preparation' in *A Better Start in Working Life*. A new improved scheme was proposed by the

MSC in *A New Training Initiative: An Agenda for Action* (1981) and in November 1982 the MSC announced an intervention in the school curriculum in the form of the Technical and Vocational Education Initiative (TVEI) for the fourteen–eighteen age group; in 1983 the MSC announced its Youth Training Scheme (YTS) which became a two year full-time programme in 1986. It has been suggested that the MSC was merely filling a vacuum left by the DES. The Ministry of Education since 1944, and later the DES, consistently neglected technical education despite the advice of successive generations of HMI, some of whom were, individually, extremely able and outspoken. However, HMI failed to make sufficient impression on their civil service colleagues about the need for radical change.

Meanwhile, the main DES and HMI initiative came through the Further Education Unit (FEU) which was responsible for a good deal of radical curriculum thinking within further education. In June 1979 *A Basis for Choice* made a number of very important proposals; it was followed in January 1981 by *Vocational Preparation*, and in August 1982 by *Promoting Curriculum Innovation*. FEU became identified with a curriculum for the sixteen to nineteen age group based on experiential learning and a negotiated curriculum. Whilst HMI were generally excluded from MSC planning, they played a significant role in the FEU publications. The new examination at 17 plus, the Certificate of Pre-Vocational Education (CPVE), was closely related to the work of FEU.

The Rayner Report also made a number of comments on the inspection of further education which will be considered in Chapter 10. It was said to be one of the SCI Sheila Browne's great regrets that before retiring she had not succeeded in reorganizing the HMI role in FE to the same extent that she had in the school system.

HMI, the universities and teacher training

When Kay-Shuttleworth introduced the pupil-teacher system in 1846, teacher training became a very important aspect of Inspectors' responsibilities. Promising elementary pupils were apprenticed at age thirteen to head teachers for five years, teaching in the school for part of the time and being instructed by the head teacher for about one and a half hours each day. At the end of a five year apprenticeship they took the Queen's Scholarship examination, and if they passed high enough on the list they were admitted to a training college for two years. The whole process, including the teaching programme within the training college, was under the supervision of HMI. The system changed very little from 1846 to 1890, except that by the end of the period the instruction of pupil-teachers tended to take place in day centres rather than in the schools.

In 1888, however, the Cross Commission recommended that universities should be involved in the education and training of elementary school teachers. There was a positive response from the universities when the scheme started in 1890: six 'day training colleges' were set up immediately and many others followed soon after. By 1902 more than two thousand teachers had been trained in day training colleges attached to universities. The 1902 Act also encouraged university participation in teacher training; students began to be trained for secondary schools as well as elementary schools.

In January 1923 a Departmental Committee on the Training of Teachers for public elementary schools was set up. The Board, and in particular the Permanent Secretary, Sir L. Amherst Selby-Bigge, were under pressure from teachers' organizations to improve the quality of education and training of elementary teachers. Lord Burnham became chairman, and the Board was represented by the Second Secretary, Edmund Chambers, and the Chief Inspector for Teacher Training, Herbert Ward. By the time the committee had finished its work the Second Secretary and the Chief Inspector had developed quite different points of view. Chambers signed a minority report representing four of the committee which recommended that a one year professional course would be sufficient, whilst the Chief Inspector subscribed to the majority view that two years was the minimum possible, notwithstanding the fact that most entrants to colleges were by then coming via secondary education rather than direct from elementary schools.

The dispute was not simply a question of time and the need for economy. It was also about the nature of the course and the relationship between education and training. The Chief Inspector, together with the majority of the committee, asserted that a training college should be concerned with general education as well as training; the minority group wanted colleges to be concerned only with professional training, hence the beginning of a long debate about the purpose of studying one main subject at a training college. The majority group's recommendation was eventually accepted by the Board in 1926, after a good deal of public discussion.

The next major issue to be tackled was the question of the relation of training colleges to universities. The way in which the subject directly arose was in the context of training college examinations. Up to this time examining was firmly in the hands of HMI, but it was doubtful whether a government department should be in control of the examinations as well as the inspection of training colleges; with the increasing involvement of universities in teacher training there was now a possible alternative. The President of the Board, Lord Eustace Percy, asked Miss R.L. Monkhouse, Staff Inspector for the Training of Teachers, to write a memorandum on the possibility of devolving the Board's responsibility for examining to other bodies. Miss Monkhouse was cautious in her response, but quoted some examples of colleges already exercising their right to offer alternative approved examinations, as well as the negotiations already in progress with the University of London. Her tentative recommendation was that eventually responsibility for examining should be handed over to universities, but she argued against undue haste. The Board was, however, not prepared to wait and negotiations with the Vice-Chancellors were initiated immediately. A committee was set up chaired by Mr. R. Mayor, recently retired from the Board. The colleges were anxious to have links with the universities which would amount to more than examination validation; some universities were more enthusiastic than others. Oxford and Cambridge refused to get involved, and the position in London with its twenty-two colleges was complex. A number of Inspectors, including H.M. Richards, the SCI, were not enthusiastic about any kind of solution involving the universities.

The Mayor Committee was generally successful and set up connections between colleges and universities on a regional basis, to some extent anticipating the McNair recommendations for area training organizations. By 1930, eleven joint boards had been established on the regional basis recommended by Mayor. There remained the problem of national co-ordination, and this was dealt with by means of a Central Advisory Council. There was also a secret Training College Reference Committee with a brief to keep the training college curricula and examinations under scrutiny: it was chaired by Mr A.P. Oppé, head of Teacher Training Branch, but all other members of the committee were

HMI experienced in training college examining. One of the reasons for the emergence of the Training College Reference Committee was that after the Mayor Committee recommendation for Joint Boards had been accepted, it was by no means clear what the HMI role would be in the new examining structure. A compromise was found in 1928, when a conference was held of training college inspectors and chief examiners; Richards announced that in each area an Inspector would be nominated as Regional Officer. The Regional Officer would be in constant touch with the Joint Board, attending meetings and calling in HMI for specialist consultation whenever necessary. He also stated that Joint Boards knew that final approval of syllabuses and schemes rested with the Board of Education. It was, therefore, desirable for HMI to be consulted at an early stage. According to W.R. Niblett *et al.* (1975, p. 59) it was doubtful whether the university and college members of the Joint Boards knew how closely their activities were monitored by the Inspectorate from whom they inherited the responsibility for examination of the training college students, but in most cases they welcomed the help and advice they received from HMI.

It would be wrong to give the impression that all these changes took place without friction. Many universities were unhappy not only with the standards in the colleges, but also that ultimate control rested with the Board. The complex structure in London, with many training colleges and a federal university, posed additional difficulties. The Joint Board system was reviewed in 1935 but not settled. It was no secret that some HMI were in favour of abandoning the university connection. In 1938 HMI produced a list of 'suggestions' for training college examinations (marked 'strictly confidential') which offended training colleges and universities when its existence became known; training of teachers had become a major controversy, and the Board was under considerable pressure from the National Union of Teachers and others to set up another enquiry into teacher training. This would have been accepted, but the 1939 war came first.

The McNair Committee

During the war the long-term planning of educational services continued, and took on a more optimistic form. By June 1941 the Board of Education had produced a document *Education After the War* (marked confidential) known as the Green Book. Chapter 7, written by S.H. Wood, was devoted to teacher training. No definitive statement was made about the controversial issue of examinations, but amongst other improvements Wood suggested a three-year course with the middle year being spent away from college. This last proposal was strongly opposed by training colleges. R.A. Butler, President of the Board of Education, agreed to set up a committee, and Dr McNair, Vice-Chancellor of the University of Liverpool, was invited to be chairman. Wood, despite his unpopularity with training colleges on account of his 'year away from college' proposal, was a member of the committee and its secretary. Miss E.C. Oakden, an HMI with considerable experience of training colleges, became the assistant secretary to the committee and took on the major role of servicing the main committee as well as accepting complete secretarial responsibilities for the reports of all the sub-committees. When the report was published, the chairman said of Miss Oakden in his introduction that she had

> acted as Secretary to our six sub-committees and has been responsible for arranging our numerous visits to training colleges and other institutions. It has been manifest to us that in the course of her work as an Inspector her sympathetic attitude and her personal devotion to the welfare of the training colleges and the schools have enabled her to acquire a very intimate knowledge of the problems of education, particularly on the human side, and we have derived great benefit from this knowledge (McNair Report, 1944, p. 8).

The committee sat from April 1942 to May 1944, and throughout kept in touch with the drafting of the White Paper on *Educational Reconstruction* (1943) and the Education Act (1944). A major theme of the committee's deliberations was the fact that training colleges, like the elementary schools they served, were essentially part of a 'cheap system'. Miss Oakden criticized colleges for their lack of privacy and accommodation for private study, the overcrowded and regimented programme of teaching, and the spoon-feeding teaching methods. Wood went even further in saying that they were despised as educational institutions. Many saw a solution in terms of enhancing the status of the colleges by developing much closer links with universities.

Unfortunately, the committee did not agree upon a formula, and two alternative schemes were put forward with roughly equal support on the committee: Scheme A suggested that each university should establish a School of Education to which training colleges would be affiliated; Scheme B proposed that the existing Joint Board scheme should be developed and strengthened.

Outside the committee a version of Scheme A seemed to be favoured. HMI were not the major protagonists in this discussion which was really concerned with the part that universities could or should play in professional training. But Miss Oakden has since written very perceptively about the nature of the problem (see 'The Background of the McNair Report', quoted in Niblett *et al.*, 1975, p. 112):

> I remember that many educational discussions, by no means confined to McNair, turned on the dangers of the substance of educational learning falling under the control of central and political government. This was daily driven home to us by current happenings in Europe. We rejoiced in every instance of independent challenge to the political dominance which turned education into propaganda. We had perhaps never been so consciously proud of the independence of teaching and learning in our own universities and to a unique degree in our schools. The resolution to preserve this independence and, with it, as we thought, the integrity of education was strong. This does not of course come through overtly in the Report as a conscious motive for the university focus (which occurs even in Scheme B in a modified form). But I cannot but believe, remembering the temper of the times and the daily awareness of the importance of the teacher in a society in which individual mental and spiritual freedom for which we were fighting was to be maintained, that the contemporary British concept of the universities as the final bastions of this independence did indeed play a decisive part in the move to place the curriculum and courses of the colleges firmly within these bastions.

The Board now had the uncomfortable task of trying to negotiate a solution with the universities. It was uncomfortable because the Board found it difficult to adopt an appropriate stance towards universities – a stance that was neither directive nor subordinate. They also found that Vice-Chancellors lacked any policy other than university autonomy:

> If anyone is bold enough to attack the universities, and particularly to attack their autonomy, the Committee of Vice-

79

Chancellors closes its ranks and presents a united front. But if anyone is so innocent as to consult the Committee of Vice-Chancellors, or seek their advice, on matters of general educational policy one finds the Committee has disappeared into thin air. . . . In short the Committee of Vice-Chancellors has a policy, namely, that of maintaining the independence of the universities. (Memorandum from S.H. Wood to R.A. Butler entitled 'The Board of Education and the Universities', quoted in Niblett *et al.*, 1975, p. 117.)

Implementation of McNair

As expected, the Vice-Chancellors were not enthusiastic about either Scheme A or Scheme B, and some of them behaved irresponsibly (Niblett *et al.*, 1975, p. 120). Eventually a version of Scheme A was accepted and Area Training Organizations (ATOs) became an important part of the structure of teacher education until they were swept away after the 1972 White Paper. In addition, the McNair Report recommended the establishment of a Central Training Council to initiate the new administrative framework and to advise the Board on matters concerning the supply, recruitment and training of teachers. There were also several recommendations designed to expand the number of teachers and to improve the quality by raising the status of the teaching profession. The report was accepted in principle in 1944, and was gradually implemented from 1945 to 1960. The new Minister of Education, Ellen Wilkinson, insisted on her right to appoint HMI as observers on ATOs. Miss Oakden (now Mrs Mee) led a team of Ministry officials who negotiated the establishment of each of the ATOs.

London posed particular problems. Despite the long-standing association with Goldsmith's College, and the fact that several training colleges entered students for external degrees of the university, there was a good deal of opposition to incorporation of the colleges into the university. An additional difficulty was the problem of inspection. The central issue was the different interpretations of 'inspection'. As described in Chapter 8 of the McNair Report, the position seemed to be very clear: 'The powers and duties of the Board of Education as regards inspection should extend to the professional courses of graduates, however provided.' The Board of Education was prepared to hand over a good deal of control to the Joint Boards (effectively the universities), but without the right of inspection they feared a loss of accountability. Universities, on the other hand, were greatly concerned by the possible threat to their autonomy if HMI wished to inspect graduate training within the university in the same way as they inspected training college courses. Inspections had taken place in university departments of education before, but the maximum tact had been employed by the HMI. Now the possibility existed of something much more like school inspections. Others feared that this would be unacceptably intrusive, since it implied more control over the university as a whole. The arrival of Ellen Wilkinson as Minister of Education did nothing to calm those who feared loss of academic freedom (Vernon, 1982, p. 216).

Ministry officials, and S.H. Wood in particular, tried to re-assure universities that inspections would be inoffensive, but in London a Joint Sub-Committee of the Academic and Collegiate Councils demanded a definition of 'inspection', and did not like what was reluctantly sent to them: 'HMI would make direct contact with all phases of the work, including lectures and tutorials, directed to the training of qualified teachers.' The University suspected that inspection was being made more rigorous on the instructions of Ellen Wilkinson. Several exchanges of letters failed to resolve the dispute. Further discussions took place in 1947, and Dr G.B. Jeffrey, Director of the Institute of Education, recommended that the University should not only withdraw its offer to operate McNair Scheme A, but should also give up teacher training and concentrate on educational research. It was important for the Ministry to avoid this, because several other universities would have followed the London example, at a time when the Ministry was desperately short of teachers. Eventually a compromise formula was found: HMI would have no right to inspect any lecture or tutorial class, and if an Inspector were invited into a class he would not report on the work of an individual.

The expansion of teacher training

Meanwhile, the real problem of teacher training after the war was the need for greatly increased numbers of teachers. The Emergency Training Scheme for ex-servicemen and unqualified teachers produced nearly 40,000 additional teachers by 1952. The school population was to grow from five million in 1945 to nearly eight and a half million in 1972; there were also plans to reduce class sizes and to increase the training college courses from two years to three. A massive expansion was required in university departments of education and training colleges, and it was later alleged that this expansion did not take place without a loss of quality. During the 1970s there were increasing demands for the improvement of teacher education, which strengthened the argument in favour of tighter inspection of all initial teacher education courses.

The Robbins Report and teacher education

The Robbins Report (1963) was concerned with the whole of higher education, but the teacher education interest was represented on the committee by Lionel Elvin, Director of the University of London Institute of Education. The report returned to the idea of improving the quality of training colleges by closer association with the universities. The solution offered was that universities should take over complete responsibility for the colleges, financial as well as academic. This was, however, opposed by LEAs as well as by the Ministry of Education and by some HMI. The loss of public control was regarded as unacceptable, and universities also seemed to some HMI to be more concerned with academic standards than with professional quality.

As an alternative, a committee was set up under Toby Weaver, a Deputy Secretary in the DES, to give the colleges more autonomy and greater protection from LEA interference. By this time some progress had also been made towards achieving better qualified teachers. In 1960 the training college course had been extended from two to three years. After the Robbins Report the B Ed degree was developed for a minority of students who stayed on for a fourth year. One of the Robbins recommendations, however, produced results which ran counter to the notion of closer links between training colleges and universities: the existence of the Council for National Academic Awards after 1964 provided an alternative higher education route. It was also sometimes pointed out that college relations with universities about the new B Ed degree were not always harmonious. However, the 1960s represented, as we saw in Chapter 2, a low point in HMI morale and prestige, and the Inspectors played a less significant part in this debate than might have been expected.

In 1967 the Plowden Report recommended a full enquiry into the system of training teachers. The background to this recommendation was the extremely 'progressive' stance taken by the committee on teaching methods in primary schools, and the realization that to achieve what was recommended by Plowden would require a new kind of teacher. At the time, the Plowden Report was generally greeted as enlightened, but in retrospect many educationists have seen it as naive and lacking in rigour. HMI had generally espoused progressive methods in primary schools, but many became critical of some of the assumptions contained in the report and their implications for teacher training (see Chapter 3).

By 1972 the review of teacher training recommended by the Plowden Committee had taken place, and the James Report *Teacher Education and Training* was published. The committee had been set up by Margaret Thatcher, Secretary of State for Education, in 1971, with Lord James as Chairman. James, Vice-Chancellor of the University of York, was known to be critical of UDEs, and his report strongly reflected that view: it recommended a new structure of awards and a system of regional organization which would replace ATOs.

The report was followed by a White Paper, ironically entitled *Education: a Framework for Expansion*; the section on teacher training responded directly to the James recommendations. An all-graduate teaching profession would be achieved by three-year and four-year BEd degrees; ATOs were abolished and colleges encouraged to move in the direction of public sector institutions; and teacher training places would have to be sharply reduced. Circular 7/73 was issued by the DES asking for LEA plans, and a massive programme of mergers and closures began. Although HMI always took care to avoid any direct connection between inspecting and closures, it was suspected that HMI views were usually taken into account, but there was no obvious relation between quality and survival – some of the best colleges were the first to be closed.

HMI and CATE

In Chapter 2 we described how HMI activities took on a renewed importance when the inspection of primary and secondary schools was made more systematic and their findings were

83

published in the form of the Primary and Secondary Surveys. In the late 1970s HMI embarked upon similar studies of initial training courses, both in the public sector and, since 1981, in university departments. In 1982 HMI published *The New Teacher in School* which stated that 25 per cent of newly qualified teachers showed deficiencies in some of the skills that they should have acquired during training. This survey was followed by *Teaching Quality* (1983b) which set out in some detail the requirements for teacher education. The Secretary of State, Sir Keith Joseph, also appeared to believe that the key to improving education was to set standards for initial training courses for teachers. In order to enforce his criteria Sir Keith Joseph announced the establishment of the Council for the Accreditation of Teacher Education (CATE) in 1984. All courses of initial teacher training were to be reviewed by CATE before being accredited by the Secretary of State. The Chief Inspector for Teacher Training and a Staff Inspector sit as observers on CATE (but not as silent observers). An even more important HMI influence comes from the fact that before CATE will consider an application for accreditation, the institution has to have had an HMI visit, and a copy of the HMI report on the inspection or visit is sent to CATE as the main evidence on which it bases its decision.

It is, of course, open to any UDE to refuse to invite HMI for a 'visit', but that would mean withdrawing from initial teacher training – as was threatened by Dr Jeffrey in 1947. But the difference in 1983 was that there was, at that time, no longer a general shortage of teachers. No university has yet taken the step of refusing to be visited. Generally, HMI visits to UDEs have been friendly, courteous and professional. There have been some interesting errors and misunderstandings, like two reports of visits which were headed 'HMI inspection'; there have also been some differences of opinion about the facts and the interpretation of those facts. But on the whole the process of visiting UDEs has not caused major disagreements. The exercise was monitored by the Universities Council for the Education of Teachers (UCET), and on several occasions senior HMI have discussed difficulties and procedures with UCET representatives.

Another problem which arose as a result of the HMI visits was the issue of whether reports on UDEs should be published. At first UCET took the line that this distinction between university and public sector institutions should be preserved, and that no report of a visit should be published, symbolizing the difference between a public sector inspection and a UDE visit. However, several universities eventually took the decision to 'circulate the report widely', in one case after some pressure had been exerted on the Vice-Chancellor by the Chairman of the University Grants Committee. The real difference that emerged between university visits and public sector inspections was the right to reply: UCET insisted that whenever a copy of the report was sent it should be accompanied by a copy of the university response. Throughout this interesting episode, university relations with HMI were better than relations with the DES who seemed to be much less well informed about the work of UDEs. HMI, on the other hand, seemed to be genuinely concerned to preserve the work of universities in the field of teacher training, on the grounds of its superior quality, at a time when financial cuts were producing a new round of closures in the public sector. Now that an increase in primary teachers is required for the late 1980s, universities are being encouraged to expand their primary courses, despite the fact that some public sector institutions are under threat of closure.

Conclusion

The influence of HMI on FE, HE and teacher training has generally been beneficial. HMI have seen professional needs at times when others were less far-sighted. They have not always been as successful as, in retrospect, some would have wished. Since the Rayner Report many additional Inspectors have been recruited with experience in HE and teacher education. Since 1981 the inspection of teacher education has been a very high priority for the Secretary of State and this has been accepted by HMI as legitimate policy.

Chapter 6

Women inspectors

The recruitment of women to the Inspectorate was a comparatively late development in its history. This chapter will examine some of the reasons for their eventual acceptance, how they were organized and the nature of their work.

Growth of opportunities 1870–96

There was a growing demand by educated middle-class women during the nineteenth century for wider opportunities to use their talents. In the education sphere, apart from teaching, there were few other outlets. As early as 1870, the Council of the Women's Emancipation Union, consisting of men as well as women, presented a memorial to W.E. Forster, the Vice-President of the Council, stating the case for the appointment of women as HMI: 'It is altogether impossible that men, however thoroughly trained, and however much they may have learnt by practical experience, can be so suited for the inspection of girls' schools . . . as women would be.' Forster told the deputation that the Lord President had ruled that no one should be appointed as HMI who did not possess a university degree. By 1892 when this condition had been met by a number of women, a similar petition was presented to the current Vice-President of the Council, A.H.D. Acland, who replied:

> The appointment of properly qualified women as Inspectors of Elementary Schools for girls and infants is a policy which, while there is much to be said in its favour, would obviously involve large changes in the organisation of the Education

Department. For such changes Mr. Acland thinks the
Department is hardly ready at present ('Practical Work for
Women Workers', *Shafts*, vol. iv, no. 1, January 1896).

From the time of the 1870 Education Act, there had been greater
opportunities for women to become involved in aspects of
educational administration. The school board, the first elected
public body to admit women on the same terms as men, provided
a great stimulus. For example, the London School Board
attracted to its ranks, amongst others, Britain's first woman
doctor, Elizabeth Garrett, and the Honourable Maude Lawrence,
who became the first Chief Woman Inspector. They made
valuable contributions to the work of the Board, especially in
improving the lot of women teachers and clerks employed by the
Board. Emmeline Pankhurst, the suffragette, was elected to the
Manchester School Board in 1900 and complained of the
absurdity of the Board of Education framing the school code and
curriculum. She later wrote, 'A body of men in London could not
possibly realise all the needs of boys and girls in remote parts of
England. But so it was' (Pankhurst, 1914, p. 33).

A more direct involvement in administration was the appointment by the school boards of women as Inspectors. The titles
used varied. In November 1873, an Instructor in Kindergarten
(Froebel) was appointed in London to demonstrate methods and
issue certificates at the end of the course. In March 1878, the title
was changed to Superintendent of Method in Infant Schools.
More commonly, the term Inspectress was used. The majority
were employed in supervising domestic subjects or younger
children, but other areas of the curriculum were also inspected.
An outstanding innovator employed by the London School Board
was Martina Bergman, responsible for girls' and infants' physical
exercises, who introduced the Swedish 'Ling' method to England.
By 1900, the London School Board alone had seventeen women
Inspectors.

The development of domestic subjects in the elementary school
curriculum since the 1860s also indicated the need for more
expert advice and supervision than could be offered by an all-
male Inspectorate. One titled lady wrote to the Lord President in
1880 urging the case for women Inspectors:

The last thing I wish to do is to reflect upon our own particular
Inspectors who are capital people but I believe a woman's
opinion about hunting or shooting would be as worth having as

any man's opinion upon needlework (Lady Leigh to Earl
Spencer, 16 December 1880, Spencer Papers).

Needlework had become an extra subject for girls since the
Revised Code of 1862 and its importance was again stressed in
the 1882 Code. The popularity of cookery had different origins.
Encouraged by international exhibitions held in London and by
the Science and Art Department, schools of cookery for training
teachers in the subject sprang up. The Technical Instruction and
Local Taxation Acts of 1889 and 1890 greatly increased the amount
of money which was available. By 1892, more than 90,000 girls in
2,000 schools were attending cookery classes and four years later
there were twenty-seven centres for training elementary school
teachers. The need for inspection was pressing.

The first women Inspectors 1896–1905

Although the entry of women to the higher levels of the civil
service had been a matter for discussion, for example, by the
Social Science Congress in 1879 and in a range of journals, little
action followed. The Local Government Board was the first to
make an appointment, namely Mrs Jane Elizabeth Senior, Tom
Hughes's sister and daughter-in-law of Nassau Senior, the
economist, in 1873. She was given full powers to inspect
workhouses and district schools, but she broke down in health,
resigned in the following year and died in 1877. There was a gap
until 1885 and the new incumbent was restricted to inspecting
boarded-out Poor Law children. The breakthrough occurred in
the last decade of the century. The Home Office, aware of the
ever-increasing number of women and girls employed in factories
and workshops, needed to ensure that the Factory Acts were
being observed, and in 1893, Asquith, then Home Secretary,
appointed the first two women HM Inspectors of Factories.

Earlier, there had been some moves by the Education
Department towards establishing women as Inspectors. A
Directress of Needlework, Miss Emily Jones, was appointed in
1883 to advise the Department on the subject and an Inspectress
of Cookery and Laundry Work, Miss Mary Harrison, was
engaged in 1890. Neither was a permanent appointment.

The first two 'non-domestic' posts for women Inspectors were
established in February 1896. Their tasks were to help men
Inspectors in their visits to elementary schools and to pay

particular attention to the needs of Girls' and Infants' Departments generally. They were designated as Sub-Inspector (Women). Both were well-qualified. Miss R.A. Munday, aged thirty-six, had had wide teaching experience, serving as a school headmistress and Lady Superintendent at Westminster Technical Institute, and gaining a 1st Class Honours LLA at St Andrews. She remained in the Inspectorate until her retirement in 1921. The other Inspector, Miss S.J. Willis, was the same age as her colleague, also holding an LLA. She was a lecturer on the staff at the Cambridge Training College, having previously been a headmistress. Miss Willis stayed for only a short period, resigning in October 1897.

During the next few years, a number of well-qualified and independently-minded women were recruited; by 1904, the number had risen to six. From February of that year, they were designated Junior Inspectors. The nature of the initial interview is not known, though the experience of an early woman HM Inspector of Factories may throw some light on the procedure. 'Dictation from one of Sir Walter Scott's novels read in the broadest Glasgow accent, almost unintelligible to my Saxon ears, amused while it somewhat baffled me.' This was followed by a *viva voce* on the Factory Law of the time (Squire, 1927, p. 32).

The women Inspectors were attached to men District Inspectors who deployed them as they deemed appropriate (women were not considered capable of carrying the burden of a District Inspectorship). Although junior in rank, some of the women Inspectors addressed educational matters which they felt deserving of urgent consideration to senior officials of the Department. Edith Deverell, a former undergraduate at Somerville College, Oxford, wrote direct to Sir John Gorst, the Vice-President of the Council, shortly after joining the Inspectorate, on the inadequate lighting conditions in infant classrooms. He replied to Miss Deverell thanking her for her 'extremely interesting letter', adding that, 'I should like to show it to the Duke of Devonshire [the Lord President] but on the whole it is perhaps best not to let anything you write to me go to any other person.' He agreed that the children's eyes should be cared for by the local managers. 'All the Central Authority can do is to advise and exhort. I will do something in the Instructions to Inspectors next year. If your oculist friend would write me a letter to show that ophthalmia was on the increase, it would afford a ground for action' (Gorst to E.M. Deverell, 11 October 1900, Marvin Papers, c. 257). After her marriage to another Inspector, F.S. Marvin, in 1904, when she was obliged to resign, she was attracted to the suffragette cause (Gordon, 1978, p. 10).

The creation of the Women Inspectorate 1905–19

Morant, the Permanent Secretary to the Board, in a memorandum in December 1904 diagnosed the cause of dissatisfaction amongst the women Inspectorate. He argued that the work of the women had been mishandled

> not so much by the women themselves, as by the methods adopted by the men under whom they have been placed: and this to such an extent that the Inspectorate generally pray that no more Women Inspectors be appointed, and to be quit altogether of those they have. The schools too, and the school authorities, have begun to feel very much in this way (PRO Ed 23/152B).

Earlier that year, Morant had recommended changes in the duties of the six women Junior Inspectors. He considered that it was a great mistake that the women should have been called Junior Inspectors, since this created the impression that they were in the line of direct promotion, like the men Junior Inspectors, to HMI Inspectorships which would carry the charge of districts.

To get round this difficulty, two innovations were suggested. First, that the women should no longer be attached to a District Inspector but to a Divisional Inspector and, in place of inspection of schools in a given area, be employed in tasks over a wide area for which they were especially equipped. Morant put forward for inquiry the arrangements made in elementary schools for children between three and five years of age. Thus a national picture could be built up. The second innovation was the separation of the women from the rest of the Inspectorate. Morant recommended that the title Junior Inspector should no longer apply to them and that they should be renamed Women Inspectors. Both these suggested innovations were immediately implemented.

Morant now looked for a person to lead the Women Inspectorate who was capable of convincing the Board and LEAs of the high level of efficiency of the Women Inspectors in securing the proper aims of the work of elementary schools:

> I mean, bringing constantly into view the notion that the

majority of the children in the school are girls, and that these will hereinafter for the most part be mothers, and that the infants need, in their upbringing in the schools, to be looked at from the maternal and physical aspect – not merely from what is called the intellectual and book-learning aspect.

For the post of Chief Woman Inspector, Morant was anxious 'for a woman with a big name'. The reason for this is clear. Shortly after the ending of the Boer War, an Interdepartmental Committee on Physical Deterioration had been set up to examine the reasons for the high rate of rejection of men volunteering for the Forces during the war (over 40 per cent) and to suggest remedies for the future. In its report the Committee recommended that schools should emphasize fitness through more systematic physical education and that girls should, through a better understanding of cookery and hygiene, be prepared as future wives to provide a better balanced diet. Morant realized that

This suddenly aroused interest may be used to immense advantage for the physique and moral nurture of the rising generation. Without a well-known name to conjure with (so to speak) we shall not be able to bring the proper influence of Women Inspectors (however able might be the persons we should employ) to bear at this psychological moment. We want to have the handling of infants in the schools, and the teaching of the older children (at least the girls) looked into thoroughly from what I may call the maternity aspect, and sound advice and influence brought to bear. There is infinite danger that the faddist will seize the opportunities of the present wave of feeling, and that common sense and a real woman's insight may be left out of account, and the opportunity thus lost (Morant, Memorandum, 'New Post of Chief Woman Inspector', December 1904, PRO Ed 23/152B).

One possible candidate considered by Morant was Philippa Fawcett (R.L. Morant to Mrs E.M. Marvin, Marvin Papers, 23 December 1904, c. 257) but he finally settled on the appointment of the Honourable Maude Lawrence as Chief Woman Inspector in January 1905. Her credentials were impressive. The daughter of Lord Lawrence, Governor-General of India and chairman of the first London School Board, she was a former student of Bedford College, London, a member of the School Board from 1890 to 1904, serving on the committees for school management, for domestic subjects and for school accommodation; from May

1904 she was a member of the Education Committee of the London County Council.

Of the seven women recruited shortly after her own appointment, six were specialists in domestic subjects. From April 1905, when the new body came into being, all eleven inspectors were given the title HMI (Women). (They were nicknamed the 'washtub women' by the men). It is not surprising, in the light of Morant's views of the purpose of the Women Inspectorate, that they were sent out to investigate the teaching of cookery in public elementary schools in 1905–6; the Report was published in 1907. It was a hard-hitting document, drawing attention to the isolation of cookery from the rest of the curriculum and urging closer co-operation with the class teacher. The Report was immediately influential in raising the educational status of housecraft in the estimation of LEAs. It also had the effect of openly acknowledging the effectiveness of Women Inspectors and gave them direct access to LEA officials, though at first visits to the offices were made apparently with some trepidation.

A slightly earlier survey, stemming from Morant's scheme to employ the Women Inspectorate in broader areas of work, concerned the age of admission of infants to elementary schools and the suitability of the existing curriculum for very young children. The *Reports on Children under Five Years of Age* published in 1905 contained the individual reports of five Inspectors. Each interpreted the terms of reference independently, so the general effect lacked coherence. This was more than compensated for in the directness and forcefulness of the comments. For example, one wrote, 'To me discipline is merely a means to an end. Sitting "still" may be pleasanter for me but it is not in itself a more moral proceeding than fidgetting. The latter is the necessary consequence of a dull lesson on an intelligent child' (p. 47). They condemned the teaching of the three Rs and of needlework to children under five or six, the lack of sleeping accommodation, too rigid discipline which was prevalent and needless mechanical repetition rather than the encouragement of natural conversation. What may seem surprising was their attitudes towards teachers, that 'the more highly educated the mind, the further it is from the sphere of baby intelligence.' This view was reiterated in the Introductory Memorandum to the Report by Cyril Jackson, Chief Inspector for Elementary Schools: 'It is desirable that there should be a special training for Infant teachers, but under present circumstances might not *two* Supplementary Teachers of good motherly instincts be as good

for 60 babies between three and five years of age as *one* clever
ex-collegian?' (*ibid.*, p. iii). But the immediate result of the
survey was seen in the Elementary Code for 1905, which no
longer compelled LEAs to admit children between three and five.
A Consultative Committee three years later concluded that the
proper place for children of this age group was at home.

The Women Inspectors were hard pressed in a number of
ways. Their competency to inspect was questioned by some
educational journals. In 1906, for example, the *Schoolmaster*,
whilst admitting that men HMI lacked kindergarten and needlework certificates, claimed that at least they brought fresh points
of view and 'will make up for any initial lack of technical knowledge
by contact with women teachers as he goes along . . . right down
at the bottom of things – no woman wants the woman inspector'
(*Schoolmaster*, 24 February 1906, p. 378). Working conditions,
too, were taxing. Helen Sillitoe, an early Inspector, stated that 'a
12 hours day was fairly common; longer ones were not very
unusual, and black-letter days of 16 hours were not unknown'
(Sillitoe, 1933, p. 89).

There was disagreement among the Women Inspectors on their
role, between those who wished to become more involved in
school inspection and those who preferred to remain specialists in
their own field. One wrote to a colleague:

> Inspection of Domestic Science is given to us as women
> because we are experts in these things in a way that men are
> not. If we combine them with general inspection, shall we not,
> unless we extinguish men inspectors altogether, restrict our
> sphere very much? We should have to take entire districts,
> doing everything, and leave other entire districts to men where
> *they* do everything (M. Clifford to Mrs E.M. Harvin, 11
> October 1906, Marvin Papers, c. 257).

Two Secondary Inspectors were appointed in November 1904,
Miss A.D. Crosby and Miss M.A. Degani, both of whom were
graduates. These posts were for five years only. In 1908, a post
was created for the first woman physical training Inspector. Two
years later, the task of inspecting all the women's training
colleges was entrusted to two of their Inspectorate.

By 1912 there had been an impressive increase in recruitment
for general and specialist work with an establishment of forty-six,
including ten vacancies. Of the thirty-six, excepting the Chief
Woman Inspector, thirteen inspected girls and mixed elementary
schools, eleven were domestic subjects specialists, three were

allocated to secondary schools, three to technical schools, three to further education and two to training colleges. Exactly a third of them were graduates. Selby-Bigge, Morant's successor as Permanent Secretary, giving evidence before the 1912 Royal Commission on the Civil Service admitted that 'they have regular men's qualifications, so to speak' (Minutes of Evidence, 1912–13, Q.8879). When the Women Inspectorate as a separate unit ceased to exist in 1934, the number had risen to fifty-nine.

On the whole, women entered the Inspectorate at a younger age than men. It has been calculated that the average age on joining in 1908 was thirty-four years four months. Of the 20 Women Inspectors, 11 were under thirty-five and two were only twenty-seven on appointment. By 1912, 19 of the 35 were under thirty-five years of age, with only two more than forty-six. The average age of the 38 men recruited between 1900 and 1912 was thirty-nine years ten months; 14 of these were between thirty and forty years of age and 22 were over forty.

H.A.L. Fisher, President of the Board of Education from 1916 to 1922, played a major part in expanding the role of the Women Inspectorate in the Secondary Branch. Up to the outbreak of the First World War, their work was practically confined to full inspections. Fisher considered this unsatisfactory as they had no continuous relationship with the schools. He looked 'to a considerable multiplication' in the number of Women Inspectors and recommended that the Board should increase its establishment from six to ten, to allow at least two women to a Division. (H.A.L. Fisher to W.C. Fletcher, 11 April 1919, PRO Ed 23/846). The Treasury sanctioned the increase. From 1919, men and women participated in the inspection of all secondary schools.

The lot of the Woman Elementary Inspector was unfavourably contrasted with that of her secondary colleague by the Chief Woman Inspector, Miss A.E. Wark, in 1923:

> Full Inspections in Secondary work make it come about that Secondary Women Inspectors are constantly in the company of their men and women colleagues. A number of Secondary Inspectors often stay three and four days consecutively in the week together in one place. They have a private sitting room and during the evenings they discuss all kinds of things. There are also leisurely discussions with the Head Mistress and with the staff during the day.

Further, the Secondary Women Inspectors have a number of schools for which they are entirely responsible. When a Full Inspection is due in one of these schools the Woman Inspector makes the arrangements, takes the chair at the Governors' meeting and is responsible for drawing up the report.

The Elementary Woman Inspector may work for weeks without meeting anyone but the teachers whom she is inspecting, and she may have no work for which she is responsible. It is of course quite usual for the Elementary Woman Inspector to have a list of schools to be visited, but this list may be, and in some cases is, changed every term. There is no certainty that the same school will be seen twice by the same person. I think too the feeling of partnership which I certainly felt as an Elementary Woman Inspector with all my colleagues is in danger (Wark to Richards, 22 August 1923, PRO Ed 23/846).

Miss Wark suggested three ways in which the situation could be improved. First, that every Woman Inspector should have a number of schools for which she should be responsible for at least a three year period; it was desirable that Women Inspectors should meet Directors of Education and other LEA officials, either by going to the office by themselves or with a District Inspector. Second, that in the case of more recent appointments where the Woman Inspector had a university degree with a subject, she should be given responsibility for that subject throughout a part of the Division. Third, that Elementary Women Inspectors be invited to attend the Elementary Divisional Conferences.

Not only does she see you [SCI Mr H.M. Richards] and other officials from the office and hear the recent and coming policy of the office first hand, but she meets her colleagues of the Division (a most important event for some of the women who during the rest of the year are rather isolated) and she hears the policy of the Division (Wark to Richards, 22 August 1923, PRO Ed 23/846).

Richards's own view was that the second and third recommendations should be accepted. However, the problems of direct access to an LEA was a 'more difficult matter' and could not be made a rule (Memorandum, 25 August 1923, PRO Ed 23/846).
One other important reform introduced by Fisher in 1919 was

the promotion to Staff Inspector rank of seven Women Inspectors, each attached to one of the main branches of the Inspectorate, two in domestic subjects, one in teacher training, one technical and one secondary. Two Elementary Staff Inspectorships were also created in 1922.

Issues affecting terms of service 1919–45

So far we have been concerned with tracing the nature of the Women Inspectorate's duties. Something must be said now about three aspects of their conditions of service which, compared with those of their male colleagues, put them at a disadvantage, namely, the marriage bar, aggregation and pay.

Although a number of women had been employed in the Civil Service since 1870, these were mainly clerical officers in the Post Office or typists. On marriage, it was usual for them to resign. A Treasury Minute of 17 March 1894 formalized this arrangement, stating that the services of women typists ceased as a matter of course on marriage. A further Minute of 21 November 1895 extended this rule to all classes of 'established female labour'. This rule, of course, affected the Women Sub-Inspectors who were appointed from the following year and accounted for the regular turnover of their numbers until the late 1930s. When this issue was taken up by the MacDonnell Commission on the Civil Service (1912–13), its members were unable to submit a unanimous recommendation. However, it concluded,

> The majority of us regard as essential to maintain the existing rule intact, and apart from considerations as to the welfare of the family (and these must not be ignored) believe that the responsibilities of married life are normally incompatible with the devotion of a woman's whole time and unimpaired energy to the public service (MacDonnell Commission, 1912–13, Chapter 10, para. 20).

After the First World War, it seemed likely that Section 1 of the Sex Disqualification (Removal) Act 1919, which provided that 'a person shall not be disqualified by sex or marriage from the exercise of any public function or from being appointed to any civil or judicial office or post', had removed the marriage bar for Women Inspectors. However, the Act specifically made an exception for the Civil Service where an Order in Council could be made, providing for and prescribing the conditions on which women were admitted to or could continue to hold posts. An Order in Council was applied for and granted in July 1920: the regulations issued in the following year confirmed the status quo, namely that female candidates for Civil Service establishments were to be unmarried and would resign on marriage. Under exceptional circumstances this rule could be waived but this right was exercised only on one occasion in the next decade. The matter was briefly considered once more by the Royal Commission on the Civil Service 1929–30; it concluded that 'On balance, the disadvantages which would result from the removal of the bar outweigh the disadvantages which result from its retention.' (Recommendations, Parliamentary Papers, X, 1930–1, para. 436.) A committee of Women Inspectors submitted a statement to the Commission, pointing out the injustice of the differences in the conditions of retirement for men and women (*ibid.*, Minutes of Evidence, p. 506). The marriage bar was finally removed after the Second World War.

The second outstanding issue was officially called the 'aggregation' of the Inspectorate, that is, the recognition that women should be regarded as competent to undertake the full responsibilities which had long been given to men only. The seven Staff Inspectorships created in 1919 had been increased to eleven by 1925. Circular 1382, issued in 1926, changed the nature of these posts. Their incumbents were renamed Divisional Women Staff Inspectors, each attached to and working under a Divisional Inspector; they were responsible for the inspection of women, girls and young children within the Division whilst continuing to work in their own branches.

The evidence presented by the Board of Education Inspectors' Association to the 1930 Royal Commission on the Civil Service clearly showed that the status of women in the Inspectorate had hardly improved since Fisher's time. In the Elementary School branch, where the largest group of women worked, the District Inspector was still, in all cases, a man. The quality and quantity of tasks assigned to women in this branch were officially undefined, and varied widely from one district to another. The women were rarely consulted on questions of educational policy or on those arising out of proposals by LEAs for reorganizing their schools and for building programmes, and claimed to be ignorant of official policy. Women Inspectors in secondary schools, however, enjoyed a larger measure of responsibility. They were given charge of full inspections of secondary schools and were assigned schools of their own. Nevertheless, men

Inspectors were in administrative charge of all the districts, and a Board directive in 1929 reaffirmed the principle of full responsibility of the District Inspector for the organization of secondary schools in his district and his position as the Board's spokesman with the LEA. Similar situations were to be found in other branches of the Inspectorate's activities. Apart from their mode of operating within each branch, Women Inspectors demonstrated how they had never been incorporated into the main organization of the Inspectorate. They were limited to matters dealing with women, girls and younger children, whereas in the interests of education as a whole there needed to be full co-operation between men and women Inspectors. They were also restricted in the range of subjects which they inspected. They were still not invited to conferences concerned with educational and administrative policy nor were they adequately represented on the network of inspectorial committees.

Such inequalities of responsibility were largely linked with the third issue, that is the considerable differences in salaries (as well as in superannuation arrangements) between men and women Inspectors. Up to 1905, when the separate corps of Women Inspectors was established, their joining salary was the same as for men Junior Inspectors. The Treasury thereafter did not sanction any increase when they became HMI. Fisher expressed his regret in June 1919 that the Treasury 'have not seen their way to make any improvements in the state of salaries for Women Inspectors.' He quoted the case of one promising Woman Inspector aged thirty-four who was receiving a salary on a scale £275 to £370. The salary of Women Inspectors appointed by the Ministry of Labour, in contrast, started at £400 and rose to £600. A more direct comparison was made with the LCC where Women Inspectors were on a scale £600 to £800 (H.A.L. Fisher, Memorandum, 12 June 1919, PRO Ed 23/153). The salary differences between men and women remained. In 1932, for instance, the scales were those given in Table 6.1.

The first significant move to correct this anomaly followed from the recommendation contained in the 1921 Report of the Royal Commission on the Civil Service, that early steps should be taken to implement a system of complete aggregation. The recruitment to the grade of Woman Inspector ceased from 1 January 1934 and with a now unified service, full responsibilities were given equally to men and women. Access to higher posts was also made available. The first women Elementary District Inspectors, apart from a solitary instance in Westmorland from 1924 to 1928, were

TABLE 6.1   *Comparison of HMI salaries by sex, 1932*

	£
Senior Chief Inspector	1500
Chief Woman Inspector	850–1000
Staff Inspector (Men)	900–1000
(Women)	550– 650
HMI (Men)	500- 900
(Women)	300– 500

Source: *Whitaker's Almanack* 1932, pp. 203–4.

appointed in 1933 and in the Secondary Branch shortly afterwards. When the Chief Woman Inspector, Miss A.G. Philip, retired in 1938, the title was no longer used and her successor was called Senior Woman Inspector. The first and only holder, Miss D.M. Hammonds, had been the first Woman Divisional Inspector, in 1936. By 1945, only four of the former Women Inspectors were still serving. In that same year, Miss F.M. Tann became the first Woman Chief Inspector, with special responsibility for primary education.

From 1945 to the present

The achievement of equal pay in the Inspectorate by 1961 completed the process of reforms. By the late 1960s women constituted over a quarter of the English and Welsh Inspectorates, with 387 men and 142 women. During the course of the proceedings of the Select Committee on Education and Science 1967–8, information on the recruitment and status of women Inspectors emerged from witnesses. Much attention was paid to the question of maintaining a reasonable balance between men and women and also of ways to encourage women to apply. The then SCI, W.R. Elliott, told the Committee that when vacancies were advertised, of the 350 to 400 applications which would normally be received, only five were likely to be from women (Select Committee of Education and Science, 1968, Q. 14). He attributed the paucity of applicants to the unwillingness of women to take posts of responsibility and the unattractiveness to a woman of a life with constant travelling and nights away from home. Miss H.E. Vidal, Chairman of the Association of Head Mistresses, believed that many women preferred to have direct contact with children rather than with teachers and LEAs (*ibid.*, Q. 779). One witness, R.R. Pedley of the Association of Head Masters, suggested that joining the Inspectorate was rather like marriage, 'One has to apply and one has to accept. So it may not just be a question of women not applying but women not being acceptable. Personally, I would not know' (*ibid.*, Q. 780). The chairman of the Association of Headmistresses stated, 'We do know that a lot of men are recruited by being encouraged by the Inspectorate to apply. Whether there is as much encouragement of the women to apply as there is of the men I am doubtful' (*ibid*).

The Senior Chief Inspector admitted that 'it is a legitimate criticism that we are so masculine at the top' (*ibid.*, Q. 14). At that time there was no woman Chief Inspector nor woman Divisional Inspector, though one had recently retired from the latter post. Miss M.J. Marshall, then Staff Inspector for Secondary Education, who later became the Chief Inspector with responsibility for secondary schools, attributed the shortfall of women in the Inspectorate to a number of factors, drawing attention to similar difficulties within the teaching profession in appointing women to senior posts as heads of large schools and to the small number of unmarried professional women who were free to take the kind of post offered by the Inspectorate (Q. 1022).

The Report of the Select Committee, some eight pages in length, devoted only four lines to this issue; it noted the comparatively small number of women admitted to the Inspectorate and stated that the situation was likely to improve (1968, para. 16, p. vii). The Recommendations were even vaguer; no specific mention of the problem was made, merely that 'the system of recruitment appears generally adequate' (*ibid.*, Recommendations, para. 7, p. xiii). However, since this time, the number of women recruited to the Inspectorate has remained steady. Many fill high positions, the most notable example being the appointment in 1974 of Miss Sheila Browne to the post of Senior Chief Inspector. There is also a Chief Inspector for Teacher Training, seven Staff Inspectors – Home Economics, Health and Social Services, Secondary (Assessment), Primary, Teacher Training, Personnel and Information Processing – and a

Divisional Inspector. Approximately 20 per cent of HMI, ninety-three of the 462, are women.

Conclusion

The participation of women in inspection has evolved in an interesting manner over the last century. Beginning as an 'auxiliary' type of Inspectorate to HMI, concerned with domestic subjects and girls' and young children's education, Women Inspectors became a self-contained corps from 1904 at Morant's prompting. Issues, particularly those of aggregation, the marriage bar and salary inequalities with men HMI, limited their opportunities to accept wider responsibilities. From the 1930s these disabilities were gradually removed and equality of opportunity within the Inspectorate has now been achieved. But at all levels women are still in the minority.

Chapter 7

Relations between DES, HMI and LEAs

This chapter will concentrate on the post-1944 period, with a few references back to important incidents or precedents set in the previous hundred years of HMI history.

The 1944 Act clearly accepted HMI as the professional, expert wing of the Ministry. That was a continuation of a long-established tradition for HMI, but it is worth noting that in the very early days the Inspector was not seen as an expert professional but as a gifted amateur – a well educated man of good breeding and character. The dislike of centralization, which was so deep-rooted in English culture, has often been matched by an apparent dislike of 'the expert'. Edmonds makes this general point about Inspectors in the 1830s:

> The new conception of Her Majesty's Inspector in the 1830s did not envisage training as a pre-requisite. None of the first four appointed Factory Inspectors had previous experience; nor had the first appointed Mines Inspector a decade later. . . . Perhaps a House of Commons Select Committee in 1835 best showed the prevailing attitude to pit inspection by recommending that 'men of known ability be encouraged to visit mines, whether in the character of distinguished scientists, chemists, mechanists or philanthropists.' By 1850, however, the importance of some form of preparatory training was beginning to be grasped, for under the Mines Act of that year, four skilled mining engineers were appointed inspectors (Edmonds, 1962, pp. 27–8).

This attitude to centralism and to professional expertise lasted well into the twentieth century, and the amateur tradition is not completely absent from the Inspectorate today. R.R. Feilden, an ex-HMI, giving evidence to a Select Committee stated 'So long as they remain anchored to the Administrative Class of the Civil Service they will retain the characteristics of amateurism which, however unfairly, are still associated with that particular echelon' (Select Committee, 1967–8, p. 260).

The two Inspectors appointed in 1839 were very much in the category of 'men of ability' rather than experienced professionals. They were very conscious of their lack of expertise in schools, and deferred to Kay-Shuttleworth's superior knowledge, asking his advice frequently and seeking more detailed instructions from him (Smith, 1923). By the time of the Revised Code of 1862, however, the expert role of the Inspector was more clearly established, even if direct experience was still rare. It is perhaps worth stating that HMI independence applied not only to freedom from interference by civil servants, but also by politicians. But by the time of Robert Lowe's dramatic resignation it was protection from bureaucratic amendment rather than political pressure which was the issue. The Select Committee on Education in 1864 re-affirmed that the Committee of Council did have a right and a duty to ensure that Inspectors' reports did not contain irrelevant material or controversial argument. However, the independence of reports was regarded as of great importance, and it was thought that any suspicion that reports could be altered in the office would lower their value as a source of independent testimony (see Chapter 1).

A typical British compromise was eventually arrived at rather than consciously worked out: HMI were independent of government, and should not be muzzled by politicians or their civil servants. But HMI had to submit reports which did not stray from the subject matter, and they were expected not to take sides on matters of government policy either in their reports or in public utterances or publications.

Edmonds quotes Walter Runciman, President of the Board of Education, to this effect in the House of Commons debate in 1911:

> The fact that officers of the Board do not hold identical views on all educational matters should not, and I believe does not, prevent them from loyally promoting whatever may be, for the time being, the policy of the Board (Edmonds, 1962, p. 183).

Selby-Bigge made a similar point in his evidence to the Royal Commission on the Civil Service in 1913; and so did the Ministry of Education Report *Education in 1949*. The Rayner Report was very cautious on this point, and this was reflected in the careful statement in the DES document which followed Rayner *The Work of HMI in England and Wales* (1983e, p. 3):

> The Management Review of the DES, published in 1979, noted the importance attached throughout the education system to the independence of the Inspectorate; and the extent to which its effectiveness was bound up with this. The Scrutiny [Committee] recommended that the Inspectorate's professional independence of judgment was essential and must be preserved and protected. The Secretaries of State endorsed this recommendation and the present arrangements for securing the independence of the Inspectorate. The Senior Chief Inspector and the Chief Inspector for Wales will continue to have the right of direct access to their respective Secretaries of State. While the decision to publish what HMI write rests with the Secretaries of State, any of their work which the Secretaries of State decide should be published is published as the Inspectorate wrote it.

HMI are independent professionals, but they are not totally separate from the civil service and the government. They have professional autonomy of a kind which is not unlimited; it is no less important for that. Attempts to define or redefine this independence are usually of great importance.

Since 1944 the relation between HMI, the government and the civil servants has passed through a series of three interesting phases:

1 In the immediate post-1944 phase, partnership was the dominant metaphor, and HMI occupied a relaxed and almost unnecessary place in the political background.
2 From the late 1960s to the mid-1970s the educational service became increasingly controversial, and, after some uncertainty, HMI returned to the political arena with a very definite professional role to play.
3 Finally, in the late 1970s and throughout the 1980s, education has been increasingly politicized, and the professional role of HMI has become very much more important.

1 Partnership, 1944–65

It has often been stated that the English educational service is a national system, locally administered. Within that kind of service the idea of 'partnership' is a very natural one, partnership between the central authority, the local education authorities and the teaching profession. Partnership is an attractive metaphor, and so long as there is a lack of major conflict about policy or finance, the ambiguities of the metaphor are concealed or ignored. The ambiguities about partnership are of two kinds: first, the element of the seniority within the partnership (that is, the question of control); second, it conceals the fact that the three partners may be, and often are, internally divided. We will suggest, later in this chapter, that it is misleading to see the central authority as a unified group: politicians, civil servants and HMI frequently represent very different points of view.

In the post-war optimism of the 1940s and 1950s, there were educational debates often of an acrimonious kind – on questions of secondary re-organization, for example – but despite these differences, education was not an issue of major political concern. During this period HMI often tended to get diverted away from real educational issues and became involved in such activities as the building programmes for new schools. The numbers of general or full inspections on a rota basis also declined. With the growth of LEA advisory services, and the improvement in their quality, some educational observers began to question the need for HMI, and a parliamentary lobby developed which advocated abolition of HMI as one of the many necessary economies. In 1961 the NUT conference called for 'a Ministry of Education Advisory Service for Schools to replace the present Inspectorate, and urges that the primary qualification for appointment to that service shall be teaching service of an approved length and character'. Later in the 1960s a different kind of criticism was expressed: HMI tended to be seen as insufficiently concerned with 'inspecting' and 'standards', and appeared to be vulnerable to criticism of a central service which did not seem to have a necessary central function. There are significant allusions to this point of view in the Parliamentary Select Committee on Education and Science 1967–8.

2 The beginning of controversy and conflict, 1966–76

The first *Black Paper* (Cox and Dyson, 1969) is often quoted as a crucial example of the backlash against the 'progressivism' in education which had dominated the 1950s and 1960s. But the *Black Paper* was a symptom not a cause. It was noted in Chapter 2 that the Plowden Report of 1967 was regarded as the high point of progressive ideology in education, but that it also served to organize some critics of Plowden into a more vocal group. The Plowden Report was of political significance from that point of view, and it also provided an interesting example of a dispute between the DES officials and HMI. Maurice Kogan, then an Assistant Secretary at the DES, was the Secretary of the Plowden Committee, but there were three HMI serving as assessors on the Committee as well as a number of other HMI who were listed as 'assisting the Committee'. There were, apparently, several differences of opinion about the drafting of the report which were difficult to resolve to the satisfaction of both the DES and HMI (see Chapter 3). The HMI influence on the report was strong; nevertheless some HMI (and probably even more DES officials) were disturbed by some of the progressive implications of the report – implications for secondary as well as primary education.

In the same year as the Plowden Report was published the Parliamentary Select Committee on Education and Science began its work, and in 1967 the Committee turned its attention to HMI. This report is a very significant document in the history of HMI for a number of reasons. It examined the changing HMI role and pointed out some of its ambiguities; it probed the relationship between HMI and LEA inspectors and the overlap of their functions; and it provided evidence of some hostility on the part of senior DES officials towards HMI.

By 1967–8 the morale of HMI appeared to be low and their political influence weak. The evidence of Cyril English to the Committee is particularly important on both those issues. Cyril English had left the Inspectorate on 1 January 1968 to become the Director-General of the City and Guilds of London Institute. He had been Senior Chief Inspector for two and a half years, Chief Inspector for Technical Education for seven years before that, and an HMI since 1946 (see Chapter 9). He was regarded as a very important witness by members of the Select Committee. His view was that the best use had not been made of HMI in recent years, and that their professional opinions were not always accepted by the DES. He implied that they wrote reports that no one ever followed up. Regarding the political influence of HMI he neatly suggested that this was partly a question of rank (that the SCI should be equivalent to a Deputy Secretary rather than an Under-Secretary) and partly a question of improved status of HMI including direct access to ministers.

On the other hand, the DES Permanent Secretary, Sir Herbert Andrew, in his evidence gave the impression that HMI were a somewhat inferior kind of civil servant whose professional knowledge was of only limited usefulness and whose channels of communications were 'a bit primitive'. On the day that the SCI and other senior HMI appeared before the Committee it was Sir Herbert Andrew who led the HMI team and frequently spoke on their behalf. (It was interesting that in 1981 when HMI were once again called to give evidence to a select committee the senior Inspectors were led by the SCI Sheila Browne, with no DES officials present.) The 1967–8 Select Committee was nevertheless generally sympathetic to HMI and their recommendations on the whole were supportive.

Several references were made in the Select Committee report to the relation of HMI to the Schools Council. In many respects the Schools Council provides a perfect example of the kind of partnership described above, and the breakdown of partnership when conflict increases beyond a certain point. The Schools Council had been preceded by the short-lived Curriculum Study Group set up by the Minister of Education in 1962 to help service the curriculum development projects initiated by the Nuffield Foundation and to foster similar projects itself. The Curriculum Study Group had, however, been regarded with considerable suspicion by teachers, especially the NUT, and by LEAs. The Group had been seen as a possible attempt to establish and enforce a centralized curriculum. The Lockwood Committee was set up in 1963 to consider what form of organization would be appropriate; the result was the establishment in 1964 of the Schools Council. The Schools Council was a free association of member interests from all parts of the educational field, with the associations of teachers and LEAs predominating. In many respects the Council could be seen as a perfect example of partnership: it was financed jointly by the DES and LEAs, but there was a teacher majority on all committees except the General Purposes Committee. From 1964–73 an HMI was one of the Joint Secretaries; in addition, six other HMIs were seconded to the Council on a four-fifths basis.

The attitude of HMI to the Schools Council was bound to be ambivalent. On the one hand the Council was bent on the kind of curriculum development that most HMI would have supported; HMI were also well represented on the sub-committees of the Council and were influential in their recommendations. Mr. R.R. Feilden, otherwise very critical of HMI, suggested to the Select Committee that the Schools Council could not function without the Inspectorate. But HMI were undoubtedly irritated by the complexity of the Council's committee structure and, in later years, by the political manoeuvring of the representatives of the teacher unions. HMI certainly had an influence on curriculum developments by means of Schools Council projects, but even in 1967–8 some members of the Select Committee seemed to be asking whether there was anything that the Schools Council was doing that HMI could not do more effectively.

It is important to realize that by the mid-1960s many HMI saw the need for change; there was much discussion within the Select Committee of the changing role of HMI, including references back to the Roseveare Report of 1956. HMI needed to establish a role which was national and professional, and which did not duplicate the work of LEA advisory services. The obvious area of activity for HMI would have been the curriculum, but the Schools Council after 1964 seemed to fill the gap. The Schools Council was, however, extremely reluctant to deal with curriculum on a national basis: they were concentrating on curriculum development rather than curriculum planning, dedicated to a programme of alternative curricular offerings from which teachers could freely choose. But there was also a need for national planning in terms of a core or common curriculum. Partly as a result of involvement in Schools Council committees as expert assessors, and partly as a result of independent initiatives from 1962 onwards, HMI began to develop expertise on curriculum theory. Frustration with the Schools Council's refusal to discuss the curriculum on a national basis increased. A Schools Council Working Party on Curriculum 13–16 was set up in 1970; when it reported in 1975, after many redrafts, it was still generally regarded as a failure to reach agreement. It may be interesting to note that no HMI served as Joint Secretary to the Council after R. Sibson (1966–73).

The other significant event in this period (1966–76) was the re-organization of local authorities. In 1972 the Local Government Act was passed. This enlarged LEAs by reducing their total number to only ninety–seven in England. The Maud Report (1969) had indicated that the size and effectiveness of the educational advisory services were seen as main factors in the case for larger LEAs. When the Act came into force in 1974 LEA advisory services tended to become larger and more comprehensive in their coverage. This increased the need for HMI to establish a new role which was national and did not duplicate the work of LEA inspectors. The HMI shift of emphasis in the post-war years from inspection to pastoral advice had put them in a position which overlapped with LEA advisers too much. The solution lay in the direction of curriculum and national efficiency. The new local authorities also tended to move in the direction of corporate management which in some respects made LEAs more bureaucratic and 'efficient' in a limited financial sense; in some respects, however, LEAs were weakened by the post-1974 changes.

3   Centralization and politicization, 1976–86

By the late 1970s some writers were suggesting that the partnership approach in education had collapsed. A better metaphor than partnership might be Briault's 'triangle of tension': according to Briault the DES, LEAs and teachers were held together by a common concern, but pulled apart by conflicts, particularly about different priorities for resources (Briault, 1976).

The triangle of tension model is more useful than 'partnership' because it acknowledges the existence of conflict inherent in the system – in fact the tension is a necessary and productive one. But it still oversimplifies the situation in assuming that there are only three 'sides' and that there is no conflict within each corner. It is also oversimplified in suggesting that money is the major, perhaps even the only, source of conflict.

For a variety of reasons which we outlined in Chapter 2, 1976 was a very important year. In the context of that chapter, 1976 was of particular significance because events of that year sharpened the DES intention to take on a more positive role in policy-making. As we indicated, the OECD Report and the Select Committee did not begin this process, but they certainly served to speed it up. At the same time, unfavourable comparisons were being made with the Scottish situation where a central policy on curriculum and examinations had enabled much more progress to be made. The Great Debate was launched and a series of policy documents proceeded to prescribe the remedy – more central control. The Green Paper of 1977, Circular 14/77, and other documents which followed also served to put LEAs at a disadvantage in the struggle for curriculum control.

The HMI role in this *dirigiste* policy was ambiguous. It is not clear whether they played a major part in writing the Yellow Book – it is probable they did not. But they were certainly praised in the report in such a way as to solicit their support for centralist policies. However, on the question of a centralized curriculum, sharp differences between the DES and HMI emerged very soon. When the DES *Framework for the School Curriculum* appeared in 1980 it had not been scrutinized and commented upon by the HMI curriculum experts; this was a major tactical blunder on the part of the DES. Instead of a united central authority front on curriculum, there were two rival documents: within days of the publication of *The Framework* the HMI brought out their *A View of the Curriculum* (1980). This was much superior to the DES document which had all the signs of a civil servant's amateur approach to curriculum. It was rumoured that the offending civil servant was soon 'sent to Siberia' for his foolishness. Nevertheless, the DES continued with its centralizing policy. *The Framework* was replaced in 1981 by *The School Curriculum* which had received the benefit of HMI comments, although by no means expressing an HMI point of view. In 1982 the Secretary of State announced that the Schools Council would cease to exist after 1984 (despite a successful programme of committee streamlining and a favourable report from the Trenaman Committee). Circular 6/81 requested LEAs to report on their progress of the curriculum model suggested. Perhaps even more important as an aspect of central control were the financial measures introduced by the DES.

Local authority expenditure, including education spending, is financed partly out of rates and partly by a grant from central government – the Rate Support Grant (RSG). Local expenditure is constrained by two factors: resistance to high rates and by how much central government will contribute from taxation. But in 1983, the central government sought further control over local government expenditure by legislation which would give the government power to limit the rates in any authority where the level of expenditure was considered, by central government, to be too high. The effect of this 'rate-capping' policy on education was not only very serious, but it also removed a good deal of local autonomy. Education inevitably suffered as a result of rate-capping policies because education is one of the 'big spenders' in local authorities and was also singled out by central government as a major cause of over-spending. Thus LEAs from 1984 onwards have had less control over educational spending and more final decisions have been in the hands of central government. Many authorities complained that the limitations of rate-capping were imposed at precisely the time when LEAs needed more discretion locally to deal with such problems as falling rolls in the schools, and the problem of maintaining a broad curriculum, a view recently supported by the Audit Commission Report *Towards Better Management of Secondary Education* (1985). LEAs had made the point that at just the time when the DES was asking for improved curriculum planning, central government was limiting their spending in such a way as to make that planning impossible.

One other aspect of financial control must be mentioned at this stage. The Education (Grants and Awards) Act 1984 enabled the government to pay education support grants to LEAs for specific 'innovations and improvements' that the DES wished to encourage. Apart from opposing this Act in principle, LEAs were not slow to point out that this was not additional money for projects favoured by the DES – it was £47 million (or 0.5 per cent) which the DES requested to be withheld from RSG. LEAs also objected to the process of having to bid for this money and compete against each other on the basis of who could get closest to DES policy. The DES dismissed these protests on the grounds that the amount of money involved was only a tiny percentage; in later years the scheme was, however, extended.

The DES bid for central control was assisted by political events. In 1979 there had been a change of government. The centralizing tendencies which had started in Callaghan's Labour government were to increase considerably after Margaret Thatcher was elected. The new Conservative government was less committed to state education than any other recent government, but their *laissez-faire* stance in a strange way supported much stronger central control of education. The education policy now seemed to be: 'if it is not possible to let the market operate in education, then it is essential to ensure value for money.' This policy clearly strengthened the hands of the DES against LEAs and teachers.

Meanwhile HMI continued to develop their own independent role in a number of ways. Their own curriculum model based on areas of learning and experience was promulgated by an important series of documents called *Curriculum Matters*: they also played an important part in the reform of teaching training; and they have continued to offer evidence on the harmful effects of government financial policies in their annual surveys of LEA expenditure, which have sometimes come very close to direct criticism of the effects of government policies, if not of the policies themselves.

Conclusion

During the 1960s Her Majesty's Inspectorate was in danger of sinking into insignificance or even ceasing to exist. What caused them to survive? We have seen that HMI needed to forge a new national role which did not duplicate the work of LEA advisory services. They succeeded in doing that by pursuing a number of new policies: national curriculum planning; national surveys of primary and secondary schools, thus giving a new significance to HMI inspections; national surveys of LEA expenditure; involvement in teacher training accreditation on a national basis; finally, the decision to publish HMI reports of inspections has not only given the Inspectorate a higher profile, but has also increased their power in a significant way.

Reference was made earlier in this chapter to the superiority of Briault's triangle of tension model to the earlier partnership model. We suggest that the Briault model should be made more complex, however, by regarding each of the three contestants (DES, LEAs, teachers) as mini-tension systems, within parts of the triangle, rather than representing unified policy positions. Thus, the DES should be seen as a tension system consisting of three differing, and sometimes conflicting, groups:

1 the 'politicians' (ministers, political advisers etc.);
2 the bureaucrats (DES officials);
3 the professionals (HMI).

Many writers, including Salter and Tapper (1981), seem to identify HMI with the DES and see HMI as part of the growing system of central control: 'Beyond this framework of controls, the DES has its financial controls, whatever overlap exists between local and central administrator values on policy-making and, last but not least, Her Majesty's Inspectorate.' They also suggest that LEAs regard HMI as the local representatives of the DES. 'It is obviously in the interest of LEAs to remain sensitive to developments in DES policy both by keeping a close watch on the numerous circulars issued by the Department and by consultation with its local liaison officer, the HMI.' Later in the same chapter Salter and Tapper address the question of HMI independence directly:

> If there is doubt this far about the Department's ability to orchestrate policy change, where does that leave its territorial

force, Her Majesty's Inspectorate? How far can HMI be regarded as the willing tool of the DES in its attempts to impose central definitions of desirable policy shift and how far is HMI an independent body with opinions and values of its own? Its position in the educational system as authoritative supplier of information both to the LEAs and schools on the one hand, and the DES on the other, is undoubtedly critical. At the local level, HMIs have the functions of inspectors of schools and colleges, interpreters of Department policy to the LEAs, and are members of numerous committees. . . . At the central level, they act as professional advisers to the DES, drawing on their network of local contacts, contribute to Department publications and staff Department courses for teachers. Any move by the DES to systematize further the process of policy construction is therefore dependent upon HMI to acquire and to disseminate the right information at the right time. This would imply that from the Department's point of view the closer the ties between itself and HMI the better (Salter and Tapper, 1981, pp. 109–10).

We suggest that such views, which are very common, misunderstand and oversimplify the extremely complex position of HMI *vis à vis* the DES. We have already spelt out the ways in which the views of HMI on curriculum issues are very different from those of the DES. We suggest that this is not a chance difference of opinion, but a fundamental question of educational as opposed to bureaucratic values. Within what is generally referred to as the central authority or the DES there are three competing ideologies. This is not the place to argue the case in detail, but it may be useful to summarize the differences diagrammatically as in Figure 7.1

The illustration provided by Figure 7.1 is in itself oversimplified. Some DES officials may behave more like professionals, and some members of HMI might have views closer to the DES civil servants or even to Conservative politicians. But in general it is suggested that there will be sufficient differences between the three groups to make sensible generalizations about them as groups. From the three ideologies we can derive different views on particular issues or policies. On curriculum one can find evidence of the politicians' addiction to standards, the DES concern for specified objectives, contrasted with HMI support for a common curriculum of high quality.

Although in some contexts it may be useful to generalize about the central authority or the DES, at a more sensitive level of

	Three Ideologies in Education		
	Beliefs	*Values*	*Tastes*
Politicians	market	freedom of choice	independent schools fees
Bureaucrats (DES)	good administration	efficiency	central control exams standard tests
Professionals (HMI)	professionalism	quality	impressionistic evaluation

analysis it will always be profitable to attempt to identify differences in beliefs and values between the three groups. Some of the reasons for the development of 'professional' values among HMI will be discussed in Chapter 8.

Chapter 8

HMI as a profession

Status

Writing in 1970, a recently-retired Chief Inspector stated, 'To belong to the Brotherhood is, as one inspector once said, to work with the nicest body of people in the world, but it is also to be obliged to conform to a very high standard' (Blackie, 1970, p. 44). The use here of the term 'Brotherhood' suggests an organization shrouded in mystery with its own initiation rites and a private set of rules. Given the range of literature now available on the Inspectorate, it is surprising that this image still widely persists. It may be useful to examine that body in more detail in order to correct the picture.

A special feature of the appointment, unlike civil servants, is that each Inspector is appointed by Order in Council. A booklet on the Inspectorate and written by them in 1970 explained, 'The title of Her Majesty's Inspector and the formal appointment by the Crown still serve as a recognition of the limited but important degree to which the inspectorate is independent of the executive' (DES, 1970, p. 9). The 1968 Select Committee called this 'a myth'. As will be seen, the use or the withdrawal of the use of these initials has been a matter of controversy on more than one occasion.

The point first arose from the provisions of the Board of Education Act 1899, Section 6(1), which gave the Board power to appoint 'such secretaries, officers, and servants as the Board may, with the sanction of the Treasury, determine.' The South Kensington Science and Art Department Inspectorate was to be brought together with the Whitehall Inspectorate: as the Science and Art Department Inspectorate was not appointed by the

115

Sovereign, they were not entitled to be called HMI. Kekewich, the Board's Secretary, was asked to investigate the origins of the use of 'HM'. This he was unable to discover but surmised that as Inspectors were originally closely connected with the educational bodies representing the different denominations, and less completely under the control of the Privy Council Office, the title was designed to give them some independence; appointment by Order in Council was a result of the Inspectorate being originally attached to the Office. Kekewich pointed out that existing Elementary Branch Inspectors had been individually appointed, so the prefix could not be taken away from them. He therefore suggested that one of the options was to appoint the Science and Art Inspectors on the same basis as the Elementary Inspectorate, but that no more HMI, bearing that title, would be appointed in the future. Devonshire, the Lord President, agreed to this proposal (PRO Ed 23/271, 27 February 1901).

Two years later, Morant reconsidered the question. There is an interesting letter in the Public Record Office from Sir E. Phipps, who was Morant's Private Secretary at the time, to H.E. Boothroyd, the author of a history of the Inspectorate which had then recently appeared. Phipps had discussed the matter with Morant in 1903:

> I remember that I suggested that local education authorities were appointing inspectors of their own and that there might be an advantage in our men having this distinctive title over and above all the advantages of its old associations. Morant agreed and let me get the old arrangement restored if I could, which I am happy to think I was able to do (Phipps to Boothroyd, PRO 23/271, 23 November 1923).

A more serious threat to alter the status of HMI was mounted within the Board shortly before the Education Bill of 1944 received the Royal Assent. A.J. Finny, Director of Establishments at the Board, remarked to the Deputy Secretary, Sir Robert Wood, on 17 June 1944,

> Whatever may have been the origin of the method of appointment, it now seems something of an anachronism. Inspectors, whether HMIs or not, are to all intents and purposes officers of the Department and not independent of it. There may have been in the distant past differences of outlook but the tendency has been, so far as my experience goes, to bring the Inspectors and the office staff into much closer and

more intimate relationship and the corps of Inspectors has become a more integral part of the Board's staff.

Finny suggested that the title could either be discontinued altogether or the method of appointment altered, so that it would rest entirely with the President. He considered that the only way the title could be continued was if the King was willing to allow the courtesy title to be used (PRO Ed 23/669).

These recommendations did not accord with another view of the Inspectorate, as expounded in a special chapter in the Norwood Report of 1943. The Report praised the work of HMI, in their triple role as the eyes and ears of the Board, as providing a guarantee to the public that standards were being maintained and in keeping the friendship of the teaching profession. These three functions could only be satisfactorily fulfilled if the Inspectorate had a certain independent status.

> They must be a guarantee to the nation in any real democratic
> system that the business of the schools is education, and that it
> is being carried out in freedom according to the ideals and
> methods which are proper to it. They must therefore
> themselves be recognised as men and women who in important
> problems are expected to exercise an independent judgment,
> and to be free to say what they think. Just in order to
> emphasise this claim and this responsibility we feel that the
> Inspectorate should continue to be known as His Majesty's
> Service (Norwood Report, 1943, p. 51).

Finny quoted a part of this passage in his submission, calling it an 'overstatement of the idea of the independence of HMI'. Nevertheless, the general welcome given to Norwood's recommendation for inspectorial independence and the retention of the title (see e.g. 'His Majesty's Inspectors', *Times Educational Supplement*, 4 September 1943) ruled out attempts by the Board to bring about change.

The question of the retention of the title was again aired during the proceedings of the 1968 Select Committee and the 1981–2 Education, Science and Arts Committee. Sheila Browne, then Senior Chief Inspector, was asked by a member of the latter Committee,

> Supposing that there were to be a recommendation that you
> should be appointed by the Department of Education and
> Science and no longer by the Privy Council – and thus lose your

'Her Majesty's' handle. What would be your attitude to that eventuality, supposing that it were to be recommended?

She replied

We would only, I think, be able to do a different job; because that change *vis-a-vis* the Department would totally change our relationship with the system and the system's perception of our functions. . . . If we were the Department's inspectors, I think that we could not have a freedom of professional judgement to recommend anything at all; and I would take it that we would have to work only within areas of defined policy. I would have thought it would have restricted the things that we could have done – and a lot of our inspection is outside the realms of specific policy. I think that we would therefore be remarkably suspect in institutions because we would no longer be neutral (House of Commons, 1981, Q. 304–5).

Recruitment

Recruitment to the Inspectorate is by public advertisement in the national and educational press. Candidates complete application forms, indicating their fields of interest and subsequently may be called for interview. The selection panel is chaired by a Civil Service Commissioner, together with the Senior Chief Inspector or his representative, a member of the Department's Establishment Branch and the appropriate specialist and other senior Inspectors. Applications far exceed the number of posts advertised. Detailed figures are not available as a general rule, but a memorandum submitted by the Association of Her Majesty's Inspectors of Schools to the Royal Commission on the Civil Service, 1953, contained an analysis of recruitment. Shortly after the Second World War, in the years 1946 and 1947 when there were many vacancies, 2,209 applications were received. Of these, 449 were interviewed and 104 were selected. In 1952–4, 1,247 applied and 124 were interviewed. Of these only 15 were selected (Appendix C, 1953).

The majority of applicants are normally from schools rather than from further and higher education, though since the Inspectorate began to undertake visits to and reporting on initial teacher training in university departments of education, there has been more emphasis on recruiting from polytechnics and university departments. Applicants are usually between thirty-five and forty-five years of age and have had successful teaching experience, preferably in more than one school or college and with the appropriate qualifications. They are expected to be aware of recent educational developments as well as be knowledgeable in their own field. The personal qualities looked for are not easy to define. A short list might include sound judgment, tactfulness, the ability to be a good listener, leadership, an aptitude to adjust to new situations at a mature age, a capacity to write, stamina and the ability to operate under pressure. The salary is substantial and is linked with equivalents in the administrative grades of the Civil Service; for example, a Staff Inspector is at the same salary level as an Assistant Secretary.

One interesting feature of the Inspectorate is that since 1945, with the abolition of the Assistant Inspector (AI) grade, all members are termed HMI. Differences of status within the Inspectorate, such as Staff Inspectors and Chief Inspectors, are not carried over into the public domain. The term 'Brotherhood' is, in one sense, appropriate, as all HMI have a right of direct access to the Senior Chief Inspector.

Before the Second World War, entry to the Inspectorate, whilst conforming for the most part to the procedures outlined above, could be by other routes. F.H. Spencer, who later became Education Officer to the LCC, was appointed in 1912 after being interviewed by the Chief Inspector of the Technological Branch (Spencer, 1938, p. 242). In 1930, the Permanent Secretary to the Board, Sir A.V. Symonds, told the Royal Commission on the Civil Service that direct recruiting to the Inspectorate was not exceptional. 'Supposing we suddenly came to the conclusion that we should have a Staff Inspector who was a great expert on the teaching of Spanish, we might have to go out and pick a particular man or woman for that purpose' (Minutes of Evidence, 1929–30, Q. 9648). It was also customary for new recruits to be summoned to Whitehall by the President of the Board. F.F. Potter, who became a distinguished Chief Education Officer for Cheshire, recalled his meeting with H.A.L. Fisher, who 'spoke hardly at all about the duties of an Inspector, but talked of philosophy and philosophers at some length' (Potter, 1949, p. 82).

Organization of work

The newly-appointed Inspector has a probationary period of one year. During this time, he or she will be introduced to a range of educational institutions and experiences, often outside that person's own expertise and subject. A 'mentor' is allocated to the new appointee. This HMI is responsible for drawing up a programme of visits and for general supervision of the appointee's progress. There is no standard programme laid down for probationers: much will depend upon their specialisms or the phase in which they operate. Within a few months, probationers are given their own assignments. An in-service course for newly-joined HMI is held in London, lasting for three days, and provides an opportunity for the participants to familiarize themselves with the back-up services available as well as to compare experiences and concerns. During the course of the probationary year the suitability of the new HMI will be reported on by the mentor. Normally, the Divisional Inspector and the specialist SI will also accompany the probationer on a visit or visits.

The probationer is moved to a different part of England on joining the Inspectorate. One important condition of the service is that HMI must be prepared to be posted to any part of England as required. Personal circumstances are of course taken into account, but an HMI may be moved a number of times during his/her time in the Inspectorate.

As was explained in the Introduction, the Inspectorate is organized on a divisional basis and HMI are allocated to one of the seven divisions in England. When a colleague is posted to a division, he/she discusses with the Divisional Inspector the nature of the assignment: HMI will be expected to live in an area reasonably near to the assignment and the location is subject to the approval of the Divisional Inspector. The HMI's accommodation is known as his HQ or Headquarters. Although there are local offices in each division to assist in clerical and secretarial matters, most HMI work from home. A fortnightly Diary, setting out the assignments carried out in that period, is submitted to the Divisional Inspector and the DES.

Since the earliest days of the Inspectorate, the nature and purpose of the work has taken different forms. In the nineteenth century, despite the system of 'payment by results', the pace was leisurely for full HMI, as distinct from their Assistants. E.M.

Sneyd-Kynnersley, an HMI in the North-West, later recalled his lengthy lunches with school managers and a stately progress round his district (1908, p. 165). Nowadays, the workload of Inspectors is a heavy one. In 1977, a sample of thirty-nine HMI completed a questionnaire on the weight of work. All Inspectors in the sample worked longer than the conditional hours (41 per week in London and 42 elsewhere) (*Management Review of the DES* 1979, Annex 5, para. 6.). Until comparatively recently, HMI planned their own programmes only subject to special assignments and centrally planned full inspection programmes. Now, HMI are programmed by computer for much of their available time. They are also involved in specialist work, with territorial commitments, i.e. district and divisional, and infra-structure matters, including In-Service Education of Teachers (INSET) involvement.

Full inspections of institutions are still important. A programme of short inspections for primary and secondary schools was introduced in 1982 to update and supplement the National Surveys of 1978 and 1979. A representative sample of about 100 primary and fifty secondary schools chosen by criteria such as size, age-range, status and location, are inspected annually. These short inspections, lasting no more than a week, concentrate on a limited number of aspects such as the curriculum or teaching and learning (DES, 1986b, p. 60). They are very similar in structure and purpose – to provide information in an economical form – to the pre-war short inspections described in Chapter 4.

Co-ordinated exercises are of different kinds:

1 *Policy-led proposals* currently receive the most weight. Recent examples include School Discipline and Behaviour, Assessment and Examinations, Homework, Information Technology, Micro-computers in Primary Schools, TVEI, the Youth Training Scheme in Further Education, INSET and Records of Achievement.
2 *National monitoring* include LEA Expenditure, Equal Opportunities, Special Needs, Curriculum Documents, Services Education and LEA Inspections.
3 *Subject specialists*, e.g. Music in Schools, Mathematics 5 to 16.
4 *Divisional initiatives*. Divisional committees can recommend exercises, but they tend to have lower priority than central policy-led ones.

This is a somewhat over-simplified picture as HMI may be

involved in more than one of these exercises at different levels. For example, some policy-led exercises are delivered through divisions and will be undertaken by specialists within divisions. One unresolved problem, with increasing demands on their time, is the employment of specialists between divisional and central requirements.

It would be difficult to chart the changing nature of HMI's work over time. Further, it must be stressed that there is no 'typical' Inspectorial assignment: each individual has a different profile depending on his/her specialism or phase, whether he/she has national responsibility or is a District Inspector to a large metropolitan authority. Tasks are scheduled to be replaced later by new ones.

Until after the Second World War, HMI were involved in the assessment of student teachers at training colleges (see Chapter 5). Leonard Clark, a colourful member of the Inspectorate from 1936 to 1970, recalled meetings with college tutors at St Luke's, Exeter, where the final grades were being settled.

> Tempers would become frayed and there would be long arguments. Should a student have a clear 'B' or a 'B−' or a 'B−−', or a 'B−− with a touch of D?' I do not remember ever seeing an 'A' student among those I met, although all of them tried to give of their best. HMI's presence must have been an ordeal for most of them. (Clark, 1976, p. 65)

Another time-consuming activity, the approval of probationary teachers, was transferred to LEAs in 1958. Recent new activities for HMI include the large-scale visits and reporting of teacher training institutions and advising the DES, following Circular 3/83, on identifying priorities for in-service training courses and the appropriate centres where these courses might be held, and full local authority inspections, e.g. at Dudley, Northamptonshire and Wigan.

As can be gathered from the range of activities in which an Inspector is involved, there is little spare time for keeping up with individual subject specialisms or for publication. The committee system to some extent allows for the exchange of views and information on focused areas of concern and the mounting of courses, and the carrying out of surveys are also valuable. Annual leave is five weeks a year, increasing to six weeks after ten years' service.

Career prospects

The career aspects of an HMI should be mentioned. The average age at joining the Inspectorate is approximately the early forties and Inspectors, like their Civil Service counterparts, retire at sixty. Since 1974, an appraisal of each HMI, covering all aspects of his/her work, has been carried out. These are on an annual basis for the first five years and every two years thereafter. In the case of an HMI, the appropriate SIs are consulted and grades are arrived at. The appraisal is then discussed with the Divisional Inspector, when strengths and weaknesses are pointed out. Promotion to Staff Inspector and Divisional Inspector is considered by a formally constituted promotion board which makes recommendations to the Permanent Secretary. Candidates are not normally interviewed.

There is comparatively little movement from the Inspectorate to other bodies, but there are exceptions. In 1985, for instance, one of the Staff Inspectors responsible for teacher training became principal of a church college mainly concerned with teacher education, and in the following year Pauline Perry, then Chief Inspector for Teacher Training, left to become the Director of the South Bank Polytechnic. Movement in and out of the Inspectorate, to an LEA and then a move back, is not unknown. Recently, an appointment was made to the Inspectorate of a career administrator, Stephen Jones, who was at first in the Ministry of Defence, then in the University Grants Committee and then at the DES. Leaving the DES in 1982, Jones joined the City University there dealing with staff and management systems before joining the Inspectorate in 1985. Parallel to this, Dr Clive Booth, who had worked in the private office of Shirley Williams when she was Secretary of State for Education, became an HMI before being appointed Director of Oxford Polytechnic in 1986 (*Times Higher Education Supplement*, 20 December 1985).

The practice of interchange of personnel between the Inspectorate and the DES, though possible, is not very common. A unified grading system at senior levels, as mentioned earlier, has been introduced which assists in movement. Reluctance to change has come from both sides. Selby-Bigge, then Permanent Secretary to the Board, told the 1930 Royal Commission on the Civil Service that a number of Inspectors had been approached to work in the Office but they had declined. He believed that it was desirable for all inspectors at some stage in their career to be involved in the administrative duties of the Board, as the experience would provide them with valuable insights (1930, Q. 9485). Sir Herbert Andrew, a later Permanent Secretary, similarly informed the 1968 Select Committee, 'In the five years I have been in the department not a single one of the 500 (Inspectors) has ever come to me and said he would like to do some of the general dogsbodying administrative work.' (Q. 18).

There is some evidence, on the other hand, of the Office wishing to gain experience in the workings of the educational system. Morant, for example, sent the Assistant Secretaries of the Elementary Branch for two to three weeks a year to visit schools with the Divisional Inspector with whose work they were administratively connected, a practice continued by his successor, Selby-Bigge (Morant to H.M. Lindsell, 16 March 1907 and Sir F. Phipps to M.G. Holmes, 1 November 1919, PRO Ed 23/249). In 1916 A.H.D. Acland, Vice-President of the Council in Gladstone's last government, urged the President of the Board, Lord Crewe, to include the provision of interchange of personnel in considering post-war reconstruction of the education service:

> I feel no doubt at all [he wrote] that from the point of view of real national efficiency the weakest point about the Department was in my own time and has been ever since that the principal administrators and the principal advisers of the Minister have had relatively so very little practical experience in their own lives of the work of teaching in and administering or inspecting schools. . . . I do not hesitate to say after nearly 30 years given to attention to national education and singularly advantageous opportunities of seeing and talking to Government officials that I have learnt far more of what has been valuable to me from members of the *Inspectorial* or outside staff of the Department (men who have spent but little time relatively in the Whitehall Offices though for national advantage they might well have spent more) than from their chiefs of the Department who have spent most of their official lives in dealing with education *on paper and by interview*. . . . I feel quite certain that it would have been more useful to the nation if (with of course now and again some rare exception) all its leading administrators had had at least five years (in some cases more) outside Whitehall as Inspectors or in other capacities (Crewe Papers, C/I, 14 August 1916).

Although greater understanding between DES officials and members of the Inspectorate, based on experience and observation of the duties involved in their respective spheres, is desirable, there are natural limits to the extent to which this can be carried. HMI offer independent advice to the Secretary of State whilst the DES is engaged in carrying out policy decisions and in formulating administrative structures for this purpose. The backgrounds of HMIs also differ from their DES colleagues. As has been made clear, good teaching experience is an important criterion for appointment as HMI and whilst it is true that many have held senior posts in institutions, requiring administrative skills, it might be argued that they are of a different order from those needed by a professional Civil Service administrator.

Interchange between HMI, schools and LEAs has been recommended by official inquiries from time to time. The Norwood Report put the case for flexibility thus:

> It seems to us that there ought to be greater fluidity of movement within the scale of salaries and pensions. We see no reason why men and women of experience, who have risen, for instance, to the control of their department in a Secondary School, should not become valuable recruits to the Inspectorate without loss of initial salary or pension rights. Similarly we can see no reason why Inspectors should not from time to time become Heads of Schools, permanently, or for a term of years, and we can see considerable advantages if they did so. Indeed this should be a two-way street, for some of the Heads of Schools would make good Inspectors. Like considerations apply to the qualifications of officers of Local Authorities, where the possession of teaching experience is commonly regarded already as a qualification. Conditions of employment ought not to render interchange more difficult than need be: what we are concerned to emphasise is that the whole educational service of the nation is one (Norwood Report, 1943, p. 52).

Similarly, the Report of the 1968 Select Committee on the Inspectorate stated 'We believe that provision ought to be made to allow and encourage Inspectors to refresh their teaching experience during their service. . . . This, incidentally, would help to bridge the noticeable gap in English and Welsh education between the training of teachers and the practice of teaching' (1968, p. xii). Although the DES noted and accepted this recommendation, it has not so far been implemented.

Edmonds (1962, p. 179) has pointed out that other countries have experimented with methods of appointment which assist in the sharpening up of skills and expertise which may be blunted after many years of service. Such schemes are found in European countries where specialist inspectors are appointed for fixed periods, usually three to five years, from outstanding teachers, and half-time appointments of two days' teaching and three days' inspection. It is true that the Inspectorate have appointed individuals on short-term contract in recent years, as did the Secondary Inspectorate with women in the earlier years of the century, but these have on the whole been exceptional. As the Norwood Report indicated, different pension and superannuation schemes make for difficulties; in addition, career prospects within the Inspectorate could be affected. For these and other reasons, it is doubtful if these suggestions for the reform of the Inspectorate will be taken up.

The Inspectorate has been proud to bear in mind the advice given by its creator, Sir James Kay-Shuttleworth in 1839: 'It is of the utmost consequence that you should bear in mind that this inspection is not intended as a means of exercising control, but of affording assistance: that it is not to be regarded as operating for the restraint of local efforts, but for their encouragement.' A group of HMI, explaining their role in more recent times, demonstrated this continuing tradition:

> Neither teachers nor inspectors can assume the right to determine educational ends. These are issues which ultimately society itself has to decide. They can, however, acquire some expert knowledge of the means and of how to apply them. But to do so effectively requires them, besides cultivating habits of observation and study, to participate in discussion and to open channels of communication within the profession to which they belong and beyond it. The inspectorate together with many others, employed by LEAs, universities and colleges or linked in membership of associations and societies, helps to accumulate and to sift the evidence and so to provide those who need it with the foundations on which to make reasonable decisions (*HMI Today and Tomorrow*, 1970, p. 4).

Conclusion

Reference has been made in this chapter to the changing role of HMI. It would seem that the move has been made in the direction of greater professionalism rather than closer identification with the DES bureaucracy.

Chapter 9

The role of Senior Chief Inspector

In recent years, the public relations role has been a very important function of the Senior Chief Inspector (SCI), both in terms of dealing with the DES officials and politicians, and, on the other hand, giving public lectures and dealing with the Press. The post of SCI is very important in a number of other ways, and studying the work of SCI gives important insights into the kind of organization that HMI has become.

The Senior Chief Inspector is responsible to the Permanent Secretary for the activities of the Inspectorate and is the mouthpiece for its corporate views. The post itself has evolved over a number of years. Four phases of its development may be noted:

1890 to 1903	confined to elementary schools, combined with Chief Inspectorship;
1903 to 1926	not filled during this period;
1926 to 1944	holders drawn from those with elementary, secondary and further education experience, but still combined with Chief Inspectorship;
1944 to present	SCI as a full-time post.

1890 to 1903

For the first fifty years of its existence, the Inspectorate had no one at its head. Administrative control belonged to the Chief Clerk in the Education Department. In 1890, Kekewich, then Secretary and a former Chief Clerk himself, obtained permission from the Lord President, Cranbrook, to create a senior post within the Inspectorate whose holder would co-ordinate standards

127

and act as a court of appeal when serious disagreements occurred between inspectors and teachers or managers (Bishop, 1971, p. 145). The first incumbent, the Rev. T.W. Sharpe, was appointed in July 1890. He had previously been an Inspector of Training Colleges for some years and had played a prominent part in advancing the status of these institutions. He also combined his Chief Inspectorship with the office of manager of the school in his own Surrey village (Christian, 1922, pp. 160–1). As SCI, Sharpe was in charge of eleven Chief Inspectors, nine of whom were responsible for other divisions of England and the other two were Inspectors of Training Colleges. He served for seven years in this post, earning on his retirement in 1897 an unusually warm tribute in the Department's Annual Report:

> His wide knowledge of educational work, his ripe experience and geniality of temperament, and his unfailing sympathy with the teachers and the children committed to their charge, enabled him to render exceptionally valuable services to the system of elementary education during a critical period of its development in this country (Committee of Council on Education, Report, 1897–8, p. xxix).

His successor, Thomas King, was one of Sharpe's Chief Inspectors and continued in the post until his retirement in 1903.

1903 to 1926

Before this, Morant had been working on a scheme for re-organizing the Inspectorate as a whole. The former Chief Inspectors were, from 1903, entitled Divisional Inspectors and were in charge of a geographical division. Three new Chief Inspectors – Elementary, Secondary and Technological – were appointed, free from divisional responsibilities, each with general control of the whole Inspectorate of his particular branch. The first two SCIs had oversight of elementary education: now with the appointment of the first Elementary Chief Inspector, Cyril Jackson in 1903, the post of SCI lapsed. A parallel move was made at this time in the South Kensington Branch. There, only one SCI had taken office, Gilbert Redgrave, a Royal Academician and former Inspector-General for the Science and Art Department, who was appointed in 1896. Following the 1903 re-organization, C.A. Buckmaster became Chief Inspector, Technological Branch.

1926 to 1944

No further changes were made to the post until 1926 when the Board decided upon a re-organization of the Inspectorate. This followed the large consolidating Education Act of 1921 and the subsequent disappearance of the three separate branches of the Board. The Inspectorate too was unified in its upper branches, i.e. from the Divisional and Staff Inspectors upwards. The post of Senior Chief Inspector was revived and the holder chosen from among the three Chief Inspectors. As in the earlier pattern, the incumbent continued to hold responsibility for his phase of education as Chief Inspector, but he now was given additional powers. The Inspectors of Schools of Art and Art Classes were under the direct supervision of SCI, who was also responsible for the organization of the inspection of training colleges, assisted by two Staff Inspectors, a man and a woman. The post of Chief Inspector of Training Colleges thus disappeared. A body of Staff Inspectors was also made available to SCI, to be deployed at his discretion for use in schools of all types. Subject to this, Staff Inspectors were responsible, as before, to the Chief Inspector concerned. The remaining Chief Inspectors were responsible to SCI for the organization and control of inspection in their respective branches. The Chief Woman Inspector, apart from her disciplinary and supervisory duties with her colleagues, was directly responsible to SCI for the inspection of domestic subjects and educational questions affecting women, girls and younger children (Circular 1382, 21 July 1926, *Reorganisation of the Board's Inspectorate (England)*).

During this third phase of the development of the post of SCI, there were three holders, Henry Richards, 1926–33, Edward Savage, 1933–40 and Francis Duckworth, 1941–3. Duckworth, as one of the Board's assessors to the Norwood Committee on Secondary School Curriculum and Examinations was responsible for much of the drafting of the Report, published in 1943. He also greatly influenced the decisions of the Fleming Committee on the Public Schools, whose Report appeared in the following year (Wallace, 1981, p. 284). Richards, who was knighted in 1930, had previously served as a Divisional Inspector and as Chief Inspector for Elementary Education. Savage had been Staff Inspector for Science and a Divisional Inspector and combined the post of SCI with Chief Inspector, Technical and Continuation Schools. Duckworth was SCI and Chief Inspector, Secondary Schools.

1944 to present

The fourth and present phase in the development of the post of SCI dates from 1944. A departmental committee of Inspectors and Ministry staff considered the effects of the new Education Act and their implications for the organization of the Inspectorate. The main results of its recommendations were two-fold: first, the unification of the Inspectorate as a body, begun in 1926, was now completed with the abolition of separate branches; and second, the Inspectorate itself was enlarged. The number of Chief Inspectors was doubled from three to six and the post of SCI was separated from that number (Ministry of Education, 1950, p. 88). SCI was no longer a *primus inter pares*, but the principal professional adviser to the Department.

The first holder of the post, Martin Roseveare, was a Staff Inspector for Mathematics who was seconded to the Ministry of Food during the war, where he gained a great reputation as head of rationing. From his appointment in April 1944, Roseveare had the twin tasks of initiating large-scale recruitment to the Inspectorate in order to meet the expanding post-war school population and to restart the full inspection programme which had fallen into abeyance during the war. He was knighted in 1946. Roseveare resigned from the Senior Chief Inspectorship two years before his sixtieth birthday. He was succeeded by Percy Wilson, a former Staff Inspector for English and Chief Inspector, General Educational Developments. Wilson, who like Roseveare, had served thirty years as HMI, filled the position from 1957 to 1965. He has the unique distinction among SCIs of publishing a book of essays and addresses on the future of education entitled *Views and Prospects from Curzon Street* (1961), whilst still in office. In an introduction to the book, David Eccles, then Minister of Education, stated that 'I count myself lucky to have Mr. Wilson as my pilot in so many awkward places where decisions must be taken one way or another' (Wilson, 1961, p. iii).

Leadership styles and personality naturally differed from person to person and so did views on policy. Roseveare had been involved in formulating policies expressed in Circular 289 in 1955 and Circular 326 two years later which rejected a national examination for the secondary modern school, designed for able pupils below GCE standard. But only four years later, a sub-committee of the Beloe Committee took evidence on the subject from Wilson and two of his colleagues which was very different. A researcher into the creation of the Certificate of Secondary Education has written:

> Wilson indeed adopted a different attitude from that of his predecessor, and indicated that he found the existing situation unsatisfactory, maintaining that 'official blindness' to current practices ought not to continue. He had no objection in principle to examinations in modern schools, subject of course to certain conditions, for, in his view, the freedom bestowed upon such schools had seldom been put to good use. . . .
> There can be no doubt that Wilson's position must have encouraged the sub-committee in reaching its subsequent conclusions, particularly in that it differed significantly from the position developed and adopted by the Ministry during the period when Roseveare had been Senior Chief Inspector (Fisher, 1982, p. 52).

Shortly before his retirement, Wilson outlined his view of the future working of the Inspectorate. He favoured an increase in time given to informal or 'pastoral' visits to institutions, even at the expense of full inspections. Wilson also looked to some reliable means of conveying the ideas and experiences of HMI to schools in a collective or generalized form. 'Five hundred private soldiers, each battling away in his own sector, are not enough in modern conditions' (Wilson, 1964, p. 136). With the likelihood of the establishment of the Schools Council at the time, Wilson regarded some substantial contribution to curricular improvement as one of the Inspectorate's leading aims, preferably in co-operation with teachers and not 'in any mandatory or hortatory spirit towards them' (*ibid.*, p. 137).

The appointment of Cyril English as Wilson's successor represented another contrast in style. He told the 1968 Select Committee on the Inspectorate of his own background as a technologist – he had previously been Staff Inspector (Engineering) and Chief Inspector of Further Education in connection with Industry and Commerce – and stated:

> I have always had a great feeling for that part of education which is for other people than the sixth formers and university students. I have become very angry in my time at the number of people who look upon everybody who does not go to university as a moron and rather useless (1968, Q. 169).

English added later in his evidence, 'without making a fuss about my own personal position, I took my degree as a part-time student in the technical college. If someone had suggested 50 years ago that the Senior Chief Inspector could come from that particular area this would not have been on as a starter' (*ibid.*, Q. 216).

On becoming SCI, English noted that the Inspectorate was strongly represented in general subjects but 'deplorably weak' in scientists, physicists and chemists, and mathematicians. He was faced with replacing over 100 Inspectors in his first two years as SCI; this presented an opportunity to make good this deficiency. English claimed in his evidence to the Select Committee that, after receiving Treasury approval for advertising for particular groups of Inspectors, for the first time advertisements were issued for mathematicians and scientists in the schools field (*ibid.*, Q. 170). He was also responsible for amalgamating two aspects of the Further Education Inspectorate – those dealing with TCA (technical, commercial and art) and OFE (other further education) – though the proposal came from two of his Chief Inspectors.

English expressed some doubts on the effectiveness of SCI as advisers to Ministers and senior administrators: 'You give advice on a topic. . . . You cannot follow it through, you lose sight of it' (*ibid.*? Q. 175). Edward Boyle, a Parliamentary Secretary and Minister of Education in the late 1950s and early 1960s, subsequently confirmed English's view that during this period, SCI played only a minor part in policy-making in the DES (see Chapter 2, p. 26). Boyle admitted that SCI was not normally invited to attend major discussions, and was not sufficiently involved in policy-making in the Department. The 1968 Select Committee recommended that the status of SCI should be raised to the equivalent of Deputy Secretary and this change was put into effect. One of the strands of independence of HMI, as later enunciated by the Rayner Report, was SCI's right of access to the Secretary of State.

W.R. Elliott, who followed English as SCI, was a former Chief Inspector for Secondary Education. He had served for thirty-one years in a variety of posts in the Inspectorate, and in the year before becoming SCI, he occupied a newly-created post of Deputy SCI. Taking office in 1967 at a time when the future of the Inspectorate was uncertain, Elliott supervised the radical changes in the organization of the Inspectorate which his predecessor had introduced. He favoured the change from formal inspection to HMI adopting a consultative role (1968, Q. 101); this change required different qualities in new recruits to the

Inspectorate. Another innovation which occurred during the early part of Elliott's incumbency, following the setting up of a small Planning Branch in the Department in 1967, was the formation of a Joint Planning Committee, consisting of members of the Planning Branch and of the Inspectorate. Elliott and Lloyd, the Chief Inspector for Wales, were part of that Committee (*ibid.*, Q. 113).

By the time H.W. French became SCI in 1972, the Inspectorate were playing a larger part in planning of educational policy. As explained in Chapter 2, there was a change of government in 1970 and Margaret Thatcher was appointed Secretary of State for Education; there was also a new Permanent Secretary, Sir William Pile, that same year. A Departmental Planning Organisation (DPO) was established in 1971 replacing the original Planning Branch and which was called by Pile 'the officials of the Department with their thinking caps on' (10th Report from the Expenditure Committee, 1976, Q. 463). The most important sub-group, the Policy Steering Group (PSG) included the SCI: its brief was to co-ordinate Departmental analyses and reviews of educational programmes and to present information and advice to Education Ministers against the background of Public Expenditure Surveys. The PSG had two Policy Groups, one for schools and 16–19 year olds, and one relating to higher, further and adult education: each was chaired by a Deputy Secretary and the appropriate Chief Inspectors were members. Pile, in giving evidence to the 10th Expenditure Committee, stated, 'The Departmental Planning Organisation has been deliberately shaped to give Her Majesty's Inspectorate the opportunity to make the maximum contribution. I will only say myself I believe they have made a very powerful contribution' (Q. 473), and J.A. Hudson, a Deputy Secretary, Chairman of Policy Group B and a member of the PSG, confirmed that 'the Inspectorate provide an indispensable input to the planning process and some senior members of the Inspectorate, in order to get that input across, play a full part in meetings in the Departmental Planning Organisation' (Q. 1474).

French, who was SCI from 1972 to 1974, played a leading part in these activities. He was Staff Inspector for Engineering before becoming Chief Inspector for Further Education, with reference to Industry and Commerce, in 1965. French was also a 'founder member' of Policy Group A and, on promotion to SCI, a member of the Policy Steering Group. As Chief Inspector his knowledge of further education had been utilized by the

Permanent Secretary, Pile, whose policy was to bring Chief Inspectors into ministerial discussions. This policy stood French in good stead when, as SCI, he took the initiative in providing information on educational and curricular topics at Secretary of State level.

Sheila Browne succeeded French as SCI in 1974, and was the first woman to hold this post. A former tutor and Fellow at St Hilda's College, Oxford and university lecturer in French, she achieved rapid promotion: HMI, 1961–70; Staff Inspector, Secondary Education, 1970–2; Chief Inspector, 1972, and Deputy Senior Chief Inspector, 1972. Like French, Sheila Browne had been one of the first HMI to be on a planning group when the Policy Groups were formed (10th Report from the Expenditure Committee, 1976, Q. 474). She agreed with the Chairman of this Committee that the old-style general inspection had gone out of use because it did not answer the right questions; the survey was a more satisfactory mode of operation.

> I suppose at the moment our major surveys are more visible and more closely policy-related, but they are only one means to an end. We are constantly trying to sample the system to see which way it is going and which way it could go; but when we are fairly clear something needs attention or is of interest in planning, or could or should be of interest in planning, then we would mount a major survey (Tenth Report from the Expenditure Committee, 1976, Q. 1454).

As SCI, Sheila Browne provided decisive leadership at a time when the role of the Inspectorate was coming under scrutiny. She believed that HMI should be involved in advancing views on the curriculum, and favoured the development of curriculum-led staffing and self-evaluation of schools (2nd Report of Education, Science and Arts Committee 1981, Q. 484). The first publication of the HMI Report on the Effect of Local Authority Expenditure Policies on Education Provision in England took place in 1981 during her term as SCI. Giving evidence to the Education, Science and Arts Committee, she denied that there was any pressure to publish, but the decision was taken on the grounds 'that people would find it helpful in their work' (*ibid.*, Q. 246). The recommendation of the Rayner study, that HMI reports on educational institutions should be made public, was anticipated by a question addressed to Sheila Browne by the Education, Science and Arts Committee, asking if the work of HMI would be made easier or more difficult if reports could be published independently. She replied, 'In the Chinese sense, more interesting' (*ibid.*, Q. 193). From January 1983, all reports of schools and colleges made to the Secretary of State have been published.

Eric Bolton, who followed Sheila Browne into the post in 1983, had a background of teaching English in secondary schools before becoming a lecturer at a college of education; this was followed by a spell as Inspector of Schools in Croydon. Bolton's special interest was in educational disadvantage. He was Staff Inspector with responsibility for this area from 1979 to 1981 and included it in his remit as Chief Inspector. Bolton's appointment came at a time when criticism of schooling was vociferous. The politicization of education had placed HMI in the public (and political) gaze and made the position of SCI a difficult one. Bolton's view, quoted in Chapter 8, that it is necessary for the Inspectorate to state their views clearly and openly, is a continuation of the style adopted by Sheila Browne. Bolton has made clear the Inspectorial attitude to educational issues on a wide platform ranging from interviews given to journals, public addresses and in evidence given to Parliamentary committees. For example, in reply to a member of the House of Commons Education, Science and Arts Committee on Achievement in Primary Schools in June 1984 on standards, he remarked:

> I think a theme running throughout our institutional reports on primary schools, and on secondary schools (and a constant concern to HMI,) are the questions of pace and challenge and of the expectations that some teachers have of what their pupils should be capable of. That is a constant concern and it does worry us . . . even in some of the very good work we see in primary schools, there is not a clarity of purpose that could then be related in terms of individual pupils to the pace and challenge they ought to be meeting (*Achievement in Primary Schools*, Evidence, 26 June 1984, Q. 5).

On the question of vocational aspects of education, Bolton pointed out to an interviewer the fact that, whilst HMI inspected the off-the-job education component of the Youth Training Scheme, there was no automatic right to inspect the on-the-job component. When asked if he would like to see the two components brought together, Bolton agreed.

> At the moment I think there are real tensions between the pressure to provide specific and finely focussed training and

other evidence which appears to suggest that in the future it will not be desirable to be that finely focussed or specific about the training we provide for jobs and careers and courses will need to be more generic ('The Inspector Inspected', *Report*, November 1983, vol. 6, no. 3, p. 5).

Bolton has also taken a keen interest in the development of curricular aims and objectives. An impetus to HMI action in this field was the speech given by the then Secretary of State for Education, Sir Keith Joseph, in January 1984 at Sheffield, where he announced that as part of a programme for raising standards in the system, broad objectives should be reached about the curriculum five to sixteen.

He [Sir Keith Joseph] , of course, has his own consultative processes, which are formalised and set out. . . . As everybody else was being enjoined by the Secretary of State to start to discuss curriculum objectives, it seemed only justice that we should do the same . . . there was a responsibility on HMI to take some kind of initiative in launching the professional debate (*Achievement in Primary Schools*, Evidence, 14 May 1985, Q. 794).

The response took the form of a series of HMI discussion documents, generally entitled *Curriculum Matters*, which were sent to all schools. The first, *English from 5 to 16* appeared in October 1984; during 1985 four more were issued, on mathematics, music and home economics, and one on the whole curriculum. He hoped to be able at least to keep abreast of DES initiatives 'and to some extent in most instances [be] somewhat ahead of it, particularly in some of the more difficult areas where there will be great difficulty in reaching agreement across the profession about the purpose and objectives of particular areas of the curriculum' (*ibid.*, Q. 795). A further consideration was that 'there is now, quite clearly, a political timetable, and political timetables are always shorter than educational timetables' (*ibid.*, O. 796). Nevertheless, he believed that if the policy makers were a long way from agreement with HMI, a longer time would be available for consultation.

Career analyses

Table 9.1 sets out details of the twelve SCIs who have held the office since it was created in 1890. Some analysis of their backgrounds and subsequent career patterns now follows.

Seven of the twelve attended either public schools or were privately educated. The first seven SCIs were at Oxford or Cambridge, spanning the years of office holders 1890–1965. Of the twelve, four were at Oxford and five at Cambridge. Two SCIs, French and English, held London degrees and Bolton, a Lancaster MA. The majority had some teaching experience, mainly as schoolteachers, though three were fellows and lecturers: Sharpe (Christ's) and King (Jesus) at Cambridge, and Sheila Browne (St Hilda's) at Oxford. The teaching subjects cannot be precisely stated, but six were graduates in the humanities – classics, history, English and French – and six in the sciences – three in mathematics, two in engineering and one in science.

Not surprisingly, many of them served for a long period of time in the Inspectorate: six for thirty years or more, five for between twenty and twenty-nine years. The normal pathway to the top was usually an HMI – SI – CI pattern. Only two, Richards and Savage, were Divisional Inspectors. Richards was promoted directly to CI, but Savage held a joint post of Divisional Inspector and SI before being appointed CI. Duckworth, uniquely, rose from HMI to CI without an intermediate step. Roseveare had the distinction of being the only one of the twelve to have by-passed CI-ship, being promoted from SI to SCI. Both Elliott and Sheila Browne held the post of Deputy SCI for one year each before becoming SCI. Without exception, all SCIs in the English Inspectorate have been appointed from amongst its own members.

The age at which the post of SCI was attained varied. Roseveare was appointed at the comparatively early age of forty-six. At the other end of the scale, three became SCI at, or later than, the official retirement age: Duckworth sixty, Sharpe sixty-one and French sixty-two. Holders of the office do not normally have long periods as SCI. The average duration is six years, the longest serving one being Roseveare, with thirteen years. Most of the incumbents have received some recognition of their services whilst in office. Seven were made Companions of the Bath (CB); two, Richards and Roseveare, received knighthoods. In the case

		School	University	Subject	Total years of Service	HMI	*Years as:* SI	DI	CI	SCI	Age when appointed SCI
Sharpe, T.W.	1890–7	Public	Cambridge	Mathematics	30	19			4	7	61
King, T.	1898–1903	Private	Cambridge	Mathematics	32	23			4	5	56
Richards, Sir H.M.	1926–33	Public	Oxford	History	31	10		6	8	7	57
Savage, E.G.	1933–40	Grammar	Cambridge	Science	21	7	4	2	1	7	47
Duckworth, F.R.G.	1941–3	Public	Oxford	Classics	23	12			8	3	60
Roseveare, Sir M.	1944–57	Public	Cambridge	Mathematics	30	16	1			13	46
Wilson, P.	1957–65	Grammar	Cambridge	English	30	10	2		10	8	53
English, C.R.	1965–7	Grammar	London	Engineering	21	9	3		7	2	52
Elliott, W.R.	1967–72	Public	Oxford	Classics	36	14	9		7	5 (+1 as DSCI)	57
French, H.W.	1972–4	Grammar	London	Engineering	26	8	9		7	2	62
Browne, S.J. Miss	1974–83	Private	Oxford	Languages	22	9	2		1	9	50
Bolton, E.J.	1983–	Grammar	Lancaster	English	10	3	2		2	3 (+1 as DSCI)	48

TABLE 9.1 *Senior Chief Inspectors*

of Roseveare it was in recognition of his work at the Ministry of Food during the Second World War. English and Savage were created knights after retiring from the Inspectorate.

Many SCIs continued with careers in other fields subsequent to leaving office. Savage, for instance, relinquished his SCI-ship at the age of fifty-four to become Education Officer to the London County Council. Not only did the move enable him to continue in employment until the age of sixty-five, but the post carried twice the SCI's salary (Maclure, 1970, p. 144). Savage remained Education Officer from 1940 to 1951. Sharpe, the first SCI, became head of Queen's College, Harley Street for five years (1898–1903) and Roseveare was headmaster of schools in Nyasaland, later Malawi, for some thirteen years (1957–70). In 1983 Sheila Browne accepted the Principalship of Newnham College, Cambridge. After two and a half years as SCI, Cyril English moved to the post of Director-General of the City and Guilds of London Institute in 1968, remaining there until 1976. This was at a time when schemes were being developed for the twenty-two industrial boards under the Industrial Training Act, a venture which was of great personal interest to him.

Other SCIs have given the benefit of their services to educational institutions after retirement. Richards, for instance, was a member of Hertfordshire County Council Education Committee and a Governor of Stowe School and Haileybury College, and French has served as Senior Pro-Chancellor and Chairman of the Council, Loughborough University of Technology and as Vice-Chairman of Council, Brighton Polytechnic. A number additionally have acted as educational consultants to a variety of agencies.

Conclusion

This chapter has traced the evolution of the post of Senior Chief Inspector from its beginnings in 1890. At that time, its holder was confined to responsibility for the inspection of elementary education combined with administrative duties in the Metropolitan Division. It was not until after the re-organization of the Inspectorate from 1926 that the SCI had overall supervision of the different phases of education, though he was still involved, as Chief Inspector, in a particular phase. The notion of SCI as a full time post and head of the Inspectorate is a comparatively recent development, dating from after the end of the Second World

War. The nature of the post is still evolving, but one of the prime functions of SCI remains unchanged: to ensure that members of the Inspectorate retain their own independence of judgment and to provide advice based on evidence.

Chapter 10

The Rayner Report (1983)

Margaret Thatcher became Prime Minister in 1979. She was unusual in reaching that post having only had Cabinet experience as Secretary of State for Education from 1970 to 1974. She had retained firm views about education from that time; she also considered herself to be an expert on educational affairs, and probably intervened in educational issues more than most Prime Ministers. One of the issues on which she felt strongly was HMI. It was rumoured that she considered them to be over-manned, and that they should spend much more time inspecting schools and colleges. When Sir Derek Rayner (later Lord Rayner), a management expert from Marks & Spencer attached to the Cabinet Office, was invited to undertake a series of reviews of government, Her Majesty's Inspectorate was included as a possible area for greater efficiency. The study of HMI was one of several efficiency reviews carried out within the DES. Rayner had a co-ordinating and supervising role, but the studies were drafted by civil servants (Mr N.W. Stuart and Miss J. Partington). The declared purpose of the studies was to question all aspects of the work normally taken for granted, with a view to making recommendations to achieve savings and increased efficiency and effectiveness. The Report was addressed to the Secretary of State as well as Sir Derek Rayner, but the Prime Minister also showed great interest in the Report in its draft stages, and insisted on its being re-written several times.

The terms of reference for the study were as follows:

To consider and report on the role, organisation, staffing and effectiveness of HMI in England and Wales, including the main priorities of work to be undertaken, and arrangements for collaboration between the Inspectorate and the rest of the DES and the Welsh Office, taking account in particular of the following:

1 the responsibilities and policies of the Secretaries of State;
2 the present and prospective needs of all components of the education service;
3 the role of LEAs and their staffs and of other educational agencies;
4 government statements of policy relating to the quality of education and to the Inspectorate; and
5 the government's plans to reduce public expenditure and Civil Service manpower.

The study began in January 1981, was completed in July 1981, but was not published until March 1983.

At the beginning of the study, four basic questions were posed: first, the right balance between the role of HMI in giving advice to central government and its role in contributing to the development of the system; second, the effectiveness of HMI and the value that others place on their work; third, the structure, organization and management of HMI; and, finally, the possibility of reducing the manpower of HMI or allocating their duties to others.

This analysis of HMI suggested the following working definitions of their role which was adopted by the writers of the Report:

(a) to assess standards and trends throughout the education system and to advise central government on the state of the system nationally on the basis of its independent professional judgment. This is its first and over-riding duty; and at the same time,

(b) to contribute to the maintenance and improvements of standards in the system by the identification and dissemination of good practice; by bringing to notice weaknesses which require attention; and by advice to those with a direct responsibility for the operation of the service including teachers, heads and principals, governing bodies and LEAs.

The authors of the Report suggested that this definition also raised another question, namely whether the present balance of effort devoted to these different functions was right in present circumstances. The answer given in the Report is a conservative one. The arguments in favour of the *status quo* were as follows: first, HMI advice is greatly valued, but its value rests largely on experience gained from inspections; second, the Secretary of State had need of a national inspectorate to report on what was actually happening in schools; third, HMI and LEA inspectors have complementary roles with no serious duplication of effort; and finally, if HMI were to play a greater part locally, their numbers would have to be greatly increased.

Given the general conclusion that the balance of HMI activities was generally appropriate, the Report went on to note that in recent years there had been some shift of emphasis towards planned national surveys. The Report supported this policy of focusing inspection effort in the way that had been established by the Primary Survey (1978) and the Secondary Survey (1979). They approved of the fact that whilst national published surveys of that kind did not reduce the volume of inspections, they did make more productive use of them. They noted with approval the HMI proposal to follow up the two national surveys with a further programme of inspections (one hundred primary and fifty secondary schools each year). This 'dip-stick', or sampling approach, would also provide useful data on the question of national standards: if chosen carefully a relatively small sample of schools could provide a useful picture of the system as a whole.

The authors of the Report seemed to be surprised by the high regard by which HMI were held by teachers, LEAs and professional associations. The only general criticism received was that HMI were now more concerned with national issues than local educational problems, and consequently it was less likely that a district HMI would have detailed knowledge of his 'patch'. Partly to test the validity of that kind of suggestion, an examination had been made of how HMI spent their time in the Management Review of 1977–8. The main findings were as follows:

1 HMI spent about 45 per cent of available time visiting institutions (and there had been no recent change in that figure).
2 The 'inspection programme' had developed as a management instrument in recent years, but did not govern HMI activities completely – a good deal of individual discretion remained.
3 But the inspection programme controlled some HMI much more than others; the range extended from 17 per cent to 42 per cent of individual HMI time in the sample taken.

As a result of this analysis of HMI time, the Report concluded

143

that the balance between centrally programmed inspections and general district work was about right, and should not be changed in favour of more centralization. They also made two specific recommendations:

1   We see a need for HMI to take more fully into account than has been possible in the recent past the particular role of the district inspectors for schools in allocating time within the inspection programme. Since most district inspectors for schools are drawn from the secondary school phase, some primary phase specialists may also need more time reserved for district duties.
2   Much of HMI's assessment and judgment is built up through routine general visiting and associated specialist inspection and through formal inspections not linked to particular exercises. Present procedures need to be strengthened to ensure that relevant aspects of all such inspection are picked up and used within the phase and subject committee structure (paras. 3.12 (i) and (ii)).

The Report also considered that the first survey of an entire LEA had been a success (the ILEA survey published in 1981) and that HMI should develop an annual programme of LEA-based surveys, as a very cost-effective method of making an impact on the whole system.

The Report also noted the amount of time HMI spent on courses, conferences and publishing. They recommended that:

1   HMI should maintain the number of inspections of individual schools, but speed up the reports.
2   HMI should make less of 'in confidence' labels.
3   HMI should devote more resources to involving LEAs in following up national reports.
4   There should be more focus on in-service education of teachers.
5   The DES should consider financing a more extensive free distribution of HMI publications.
6   There should be more extended experiments with LEAs, the collaboration with the five LEAs involved in *Curriculum 11 to 16* being regarded as a good model.

Chapter 4 of the Report returned to the issue which we have raised many times in this book: namely, the relation between

HMI and LEA advisers. It was noted that there were roughly four times as many inspectors and advisers in LEAs as there were HMI, and that their roles had always been regarded as complementary. LEA inspectors spend less time on inspections and are more involved in the appointment and promotion of teachers, the supervision of probationers, the co-ordination of in-service courses, and the allocation of resources for curriculum development. Any attempt to involve LEA advisers in more inspections or teacher appraisal would probably be resisted. The Report recommended that the idea of partnership needed to be developed and that HMI should consider publishing a statement of policy clarifying the role of Inspectors nationally and locally. This advice was acted upon very quickly, and a brief document appeared in 1983: *HMI Today: Standards in Education*.

In Chapter 5 the Report looked at HMI from the perspective of the DES – to what extent was the work of HMI essential in providing advice to government? How is the raw material of reports converted into valuable judgments? Do the Department and Ministers receive the advice they need? Could the system be improved?

The Report painted a generally favourable picture of HMI links with the DES and stressed a number of ways in which DES branches were completely dependent on HMI professional advice. Nevertheless, several suggestions for improvements were made. The Management Review of the DES had recommended in 1977 a number of improvements in relations with HMI; as a result, in December 1979 a policy group chaired by the SCI was established – the Policy Group for Inspection (PGI). The Report commended this development, but suggested that the group should be smaller and more precisely programmed. They also recommended more interchange of ideas and personnel on DES and HMI committees. Some of these criticisms would seem to be directed at DES rather than HMI, particularly with a view to the DES making more efficient use of HMI time and expertise.

On the question of organization and management, the Report was equally supportive. It did not recommend a reduction in the number of divisions or the HMI within them, but approved the previous re-organization from ten to seven divisions. In terms of the national structure the Report supported the *status quo* for phase and subject organizations, but recommended that the number of Chief Inspectors should be increased to seven. This suggestion was accepted willingly by HMI, but was not used in the way recommended, namely to have a CI for 16–19 education. In other respects the complex structure was left largely unchanged.

One further suggestion was that inspection reports should be made use of by phase and subject Staff Inspectors rather than being regarded as single purpose exercises.

The Report commented on the fact that HMI was divided into two largely distinct groups. There were about 290 HMI dealing mainly with schools, and another 110 concerned with higher and further education. The two groups seemed to have retained separate identities and practices, but it was now desirable to bring them closer together. The 16–19 age group presented a number of problems and potential developments spanning both sections, and it would be increasingly important for all HMI to co-operate in addressing the issue of education 16–19.

The Report went further and recommended the appointment of an additional CI to take charge of co-ordination 16–19, and thus relieve the SCI of that responsibility. However, that particular recommendation was not exactly followed: an extra CI was appointed but not specifically for 16–19. The Report also commented on the arrangements for Advanced Course Approval. Since 1944 HMI had been involved in Course Approval in further education colleges, and the existing system had been in operation since 1957: seven Regional Staff Inspectors (RSI) were responsible in their Divisions for granting or withholding approval on behalf of the Secretary of State for all new or replacement full-time and sandwich courses, as well as all part-time degree courses in AFE.

The Report noted the widespread dissatisfaction about this aspect of HMI responsibilities. Since the course approval system was, strictly speaking, outside their terms of reference, the authors of the Report did not make any recommendation, but they were clearly of the view that HMI involvement needed to be reduced, not least because it interfered with the major HMI role of giving professional advice. Earlier in the Report (3.19) it had been observed that HMI tended to make fewer inspections in FHE than in schools (although the detailed statistics were, unfortunately, lacking). From the Management Review in 1977 it was recalled that FE Inspectors spent only about 34 per cent of their time on visits compared with the figure of 40 per cent for HMI concerned with schools. The Report also drew attention to the fact that there were fewer significant publications produced by HMI on FHE (only two since 1973). It recommended that the recording of information should be systematized and improved; and that there should be a clearer definition of the role of the College General Inspector.

Whilst commenting on the high quality of HMI, the Report

repeated a suggestion made by the Select Committee in 1968: that there should be periods of interchange between HMI and LEA personnel. It does not seem likely that this recommendation will be much acted upon since HMI still tend to regard themselves as an elite corps, and there would be more practical difficulties involved.

The final chapter of the Report dealt with the effectiveness of HMI. The difficulty of assessing effectiveness in conventional managerial terms was acknowledged, but the role of HMI was declared to be of crucial importance in policy development. The need for professional advice was stressed – particularly in the areas of curriculum, special education and LEA re-organization plans.

In conclusion, the Report recommended five areas of future priority: closer co-operation between HMI and LEAs; a planned programme of reports on LEAs; follow-up inspections to the national survey; closer relations between HMI concerned with schools and those responsible for FHE; and finally, national surveys of sub-degree level work in FHE and also of teacher training. training.

Summary

HMI were relieved and gratified to receive a Report which was regarded as 'a clean bill of health'; they might have expected hostile criticisms, recommendations for reduction in size or even complete abolition. Instead, the Report recommended strengthening the HMI position and effectively protected them from further attacks in the difficult years of the mid-1980s. HMI emerged stronger and with improved morale. Although the report was somewhat equivocal about the separate identities of HMI and DES, great stress was laid on the principles of professional independence and professional judgment.

In the years immediately following Rayner, changes in HMI practices made them not only more visible but also more vulnerable politically. Since January 1983 all HMI reports have been published. Although it was the Secretary of State's decision to publish reports, it had the support of the SCI and other senior Inspectors. Most educationists have welcomed this gesture towards open government in education, but it has had the effect of making the work of HMI liable to public debate. It was not very long before HMI were involved in controversy, and controversy of a political kind.

Reference was made in Chapter 2 to the HMI Annual Review

of LEA expenditure which provided evidence about the connection between under-spending in LEAs and low standards of educational provision. HMI were not criticizing government policy, but some suggested that they were providing the ammunition for those who were. In 1983 further political problems arose when the HMI report on Sutton was published which criticized that Conservative LEA for very traditional teaching methods as well as under-spending. A year later the Tory county of Norfolk was also criticized in the inspection report for a combination of low spending and low standards. The predictable counter-attack questioned the appropriateness of HMI methods and criteria, and also suggested political bias.

In January 1985 the SCI, Eric Bolton, took the unusual step of defending HMI practices publicly at a Conference of National Association of Teachers in Further and Higher Education. It was perhaps fortunate that not all the criticisms of HMI reports came from the political right: when an unfavourable report on Haringey was published the HMI were accused of racism, and when the report on North London Polytechnic was not completely favourable, HMI were accused of right-wing bias. In the speech referred to above, the SCI was careful to distinguish between the HMI constitutional independence from government policy which could not possibly exist, and professional independence of judgment and reporting which had to continue if HMI were to preserve their essential and unique place within the education service.

To some extent HMI inspect what they are told to inspect – but the judgment involved is theirs not that of their political masters. In February 1983, for example, 'Write First Time', a small adult literacy organization, printed a poem about the Prime Minister which Sir Keith Joseph regarded as offensive: he, therefore, requested HMI to investigate the group and to report back. Given such instructions from the Secretary of State HMI have to comply, but they do not have to give the Secretary of State the answer he wants. That was also the outcome when HMI were told to visit the North London Polytechnic: they did not find the Marxist bias they were told to look for, but they did make other criticisms about standards. Such political disputes are likely to increase when inspections are followed by published reports which can be publicly questioned and challenged.

The future

The publication of the Rayner Report and its acceptance by government ensures the secure future of HMI for some time. But what kind of future?

Some clues are provided by the recommendations included in the Report itself: for example, the possible extension of the programme of LEA inspections; a continuing flow of HMI publications to disseminate policy and good practice. The Inspectorate is also larger now than in pre-Rayner times: between 1982 and 1985 the number of HMI increased by about 100 from 390 to 490 (the 100 includes about forty posts unfilled at the time of the Rayner Report). The increase in numbers is concentrated in FHE, especially teacher training which has increased from 100 to nearly 150, in order to cope with the pre-CATE inspections.

Some HMI activities are likely to be more carefully programmed from the centre, leaving less time for divisional initiatives and problems; and HMI are already increasingly computerized. One danger to be avoided is that of becoming more bureaucratized as DES inspectors rather than as an independent body. The spirit of independence is very much alive, and it will need to be carefully nurtured in the future. As education becomes increasingly politicized, the independent professional voice of HMI will be needed more than ever.

Chapter 11

Summary and conclusions

We have tried to outline, very briefly, the present position of HMI and how the Inspectorate has changed and developed since 1839. In producing that outline we have identified a number of issues and controversies, each of which we would like to summarize and discuss in this final section. The unique institution of HMI has shown itself to be sufficiently flexible to survive in the face of many educational changes.

1 The unique role of HMI

HMI developed in the first half of the nineteenth century when there were no local education advisers or inspectors. One of the suggestions which has emerged on a number of occasions in the twentieth century is whether there is still a need for HMI now that all LEAs have advisory services performing some of the functions which were originally associated with HMI; an alternative way of looking at this question is to examine the similarities and differences between HMI and local advisory services with a view to determining whether there is a unique HMI role.

It has been suggested in earlier chapters that although there is inevitably some overlap of functions between LEA inspectors and HMI, there is a need for both: HMI possess certain distinct features which justify their continued existence. But it is still necessary to argue the case: as recently as September 1984 SCI Eric Bolton found it helpful to reassure the National Association of Inspectors and Educational Advisers that there was no plan to hand over local inspections to them nor for HMI to take over

150

their local advisory duties: the SCI emphasized the importance of the 'eyes and ears of the central authority' role of HMI which was quite distinct from the main function of local advisory services (*Times Educational Supplement*, 28 September 1984). The national role of HMI is crucial for a number of reasons which will be discussed below, but it will always be important to keep this question under review and to avoid unnecessary duplication. It will also be important to emphasize the partnership relationship between HMI and LEAs.

2 The independence of HMI

One of the advantages of a national Inspectorate is that it can, and should, remain outside the realms of party politics. In recent years there has been a tendency for education to become increasingly politicized, and it would be easy for HMI to be used by the government of the day for the implementation of political doctrines. It is most important that HMI retain their traditional independence in such matters, and also that they use their ability to pursue lines of enquiry even if these are liable to cast doubt upon some aspects of government policy. But at a time when educational issues are controversial it becomes increasingly necessary for HMI to support their views with good evidence. Thus HMI have tended to be concerned to improve the quality and quantity of their data bases. Another important change of practice has been the decision to publish HMI reports; since the publication of these reports there has also been a growing emphasis on improving methods of data collection and evaluation. It will be important to continue with the search for superior methodology.

3 HMI as professional educationists

A related point is that HMI are needed as the professionals within the central authority. One of the problems with education is that nearly everyone considers himself or herself to be an expert on the subject. Civil servants and politicians are therefore tempted to interfere in, and pronounce upon, educational matters in a much less inhibited way than they would where medical or technical expertise were involved. HMI serve to constrain this tendency to some extent, although they are sometimes less successful than other professional educationists would wish.

There are a number of other ways in which the professional expertise of HMI should be stressed. For example, very little has been said in this book about the HMI role in organizing courses for teachers, although this is an important aspect of their work. In recent years HMI have also been concerned with the in-service education of teachers at a planning level as well as in the more traditional role of course provision. Provided that finances can be made available, the post-1987 in-service arrangements will have moved a long way in the direction of a national policy locally administered, and much of the credit for any improvements will be due to HMI. One danger of overemphasizing the 'eyes and ears' aspect of HMI role is that the pastoral and staff development activities may be neglected. There is a possible conflict here, and it is hoped that HMI will resolve the conflict without allowing a deterioration of their pastoral and advisory services. An important corollary to this is that HMI, in order to retain their credibility as professionals, need to make adequate arrangements for their own professional development. In this respect we have pointed out here the less than adequate arrangements for study and study leave which currently operate for HMI.

4 Planning

Since the mid-1970s the DES has moved in the direction of long-term educational planning. At the same time it has been recognized that HMI have a legitimate part to play in educational planning and policy-making. Not only do HMI serve on internal DES planning committees, but they have continued to make contributions to the work of national advisory bodies such as the Advisory Committee on the Supply and Education of Teachers (ACSET). They have also produced documents for discussion in such changing fields as teacher education. Over the years Inspectors have tended to be recruited as specialists rather than as general inspectors of schools; this tendency is likely to increase, but a key function of the Inspectorate as a whole and individual HMI is to retain a general, holistic view of the education service. A balance between specialized knowledge and overall understanding is an essential aspect of a central Inspectorate, not least for planning purposes.

5 Curriculum

Perhaps the most important example of educational planning for HMI has been the field of curriculum development. Here HMI have made significant contributions to the theory and practice of curriculum studies. As early as the beginning of the 1970s HMI were working in the emerging field of curriculum, and this is one area where specialist knowledge has been deliberately developed within the Inspectorate. HMI have produced national guidelines on the school curriculum, in the form of the series of booklets *Curriculum Matters*. It is now generally accepted within the education service that some kind of national guidelines are desirable, but that they should be produced by professional educationists rather than by politicians or civil servants. In the absence of any such national body as the Schools Council, HMI have a very clear role to play within the central authority. This is an area where they will need to continue to guard against political interference and bureaucratic insensitivity to educational matters.

6 Standards

One of the traditional HMI roles which has survived is the responsibility for monitoring educational standards. There has always been a concern not simply to report on standards but to change standards, both in the sense of making standards more appropriate, and of improving the overall quality of the educational service. In recent years the whole question of standards has been controversial, and HMI have been able to demonstrate their key position. Their reports on schools and LEAs have provided essential evidence in the debate about standards and the reasons for some kinds of inadequate provision.

Evidence of a different kind about standards and the question of changing standards over time has been provided by the Assessment of Performance Unit (APU). The APU was established in 1974 and from the beginning HMI have made significant contributions to its work. To do justice to the complexities and the problems of the APU would require a separate book, but something of the HMI influence should be noted here. From 1974 HMI have been seconded to the APU and have ensured its

153

efficient operation. They have also contributed to discussions of the theoretical underpinning of APU (Kay, 1975), and to the transformation of APU from a potentially distorting testing machine to a positive means of improving teaching and learning (Lawton, 1984).

The question of standards is closely related to other aspects of planning in education, and HMI are in a very strong position to influence policy as well as to illustrate the general debate. This is one clear example of their national role which could not be covered by LEA inspectors, however knowledgeable and efficient they might be. It is also an interesting illustration of the need for a national Inspectorate to make comparisons between LEAs as well as to monitor standards over time. Here again HMI should review and improve their methods and the quality of their evidence; despite what has been said about the HMI contribution to APU on the positive side, some critics of APU might include HMI in their general criticisms of APU methodology (Goldstein and Blinkhorn, 1977).

7 The size of HMI

Another theme which has continued to be of interest and concern throughout the twentieth century has been the question of the size of the Inspectorate in England. Appendix II shows how numbers rose steadily throughout the nineteenth century, and eventually levelled off at a figure of about 500. Given the existence of LEA inspectors it has generally been suggested that the figure is now about right. Yet HMI have continued to collect additional duties and to expand their involvement in existing responsibilities such as higher education and teacher education, to such an extent that some HMI are now clearly over-burdened.

Other bodies such as the Manpower Services Commission (MSC) have not only become involved in education and training, but have set up their own force of inspectors. Whereas a major strand of nineteenth- and early twentieth-century educational history was the consolidation of educational services under the supervision of a single central authority with one central Inspectorate, a strange feature of the 1970s and 1980s has been for others such as the Department of Employment to stretch the concept of training to such an extent that they encroach upon educational administration. Meanwhile HMI have inspected some aspects of the educational activities funded by MSC including TVEI; dispassionate observers have to note with regret not only the overlap of functions but also the lack of co-operation, and even the rivalry existing between the established central authority and the ambitious newcomers on the educational scene.

Although a good deal of progress has been made in defining the role of HMI in the Rayner Report and elsewhere, there is still a need for clear definitions which would be related to a policy on numbers. In discussing the future of HMI and the numerical strength of the Inspectorate, one factor rarely mentioned is that in Scotland HMI are *pro rata* roughly twice as numerous in relation to the number of teachers. This is not to recommend a significant increase in HMI establishment, but simply an indication that if HMI are to retain their traditional professional roles, together with increasing responsibilities, then reasonable limits must be set to the tasks which they undertake.

8 The danger of centralism

A good deal has been written about the dangers of centralism in education, and the tendency in recent years for the DES to increase its powers of control. The role of HMI in this is crucial: where more central influence is desirable HMI can give essential advice; but there may be occasions when some centralist proposals are not justifiable, and if so, HMI should not hesitate to throw their weight behind professionalism in opposing the bureaucratic machine. The least desirable possibility for the future is that HMI might simply become part of the bureaucratic machine. As this book has shown, so far that possibility has been avoided.

Appendix 1

HMI: Some significant dates

1833	House of Commons grant of £20,000 for building school houses for education of the poor.
1839	Committee of the Privy Council on Education established. Secretary, Dr J. P. Kay (later Kay-Shuttleworth). First two HMIs appointed Rev. John Allen (National Society) and H.S. Tremenheere (British and Foreign School Society). *Instructions to Inspectors* issued.
1840	Concordat. Archbishops to be consulted before HMI appointed to inspect Anglican schools. Published as a *Minute* of the Committee of Council 16 July.
1844	Five new inspectors: four Church of England and one British Society replacing Tremenheere.
1846	*Minutes*: pupil-teacher system. Annual conference of Inspectors began.
1848	First Dissenter appointed, J. D. Morrell. England divided between the two Nonconformist HMIs.
1849	First Roman Catholic appointed, T. W. Marshall. First Inspector of training colleges, F. C. Cook. 16 HMI in service.
1850	First two *Assistant Inspectors* appointed (same social group as HMI). Four by 1851; eleven in 1854.
1853	Department of Art and Science established with its own Inspectorate.
1854–7	Attacks by teachers on type of inspector appointed.
1856	Education Department of Privy Council created.
1858	Annual Conference of Inspectors. Chaired by Vice-President, Adderley, not allowed to vote on discussions of government educational policy.

1859 Annual conferences terminated by Lowe.

1858–61 *Newcastle Commission.* By 1861, thirty-six HMI and twenty-four Assistant Inspectors.

1860 *Minutes and Regulations* of Committee of Privy Council now in the form of a *Code* and submitted to both Houses.

1861 *Revised Code.* Grants dependent on examination of each scholar: withdrawn.

1862 *Revised Code.* Grants now partly dependent on examination and partly on attendance. All Assistant Inspectors become full inspectors. Now forty-eight HMI.

Instructions to Inspectors
General reports alternate years, not annually.

HMI and the Revised Code

	In favour	Against
Anglicans	17	8
British and Wesleyan	5	2
Roman Catholic	2	0
Total	24	10

N.B. 12 gave no opinion.

£50 p.a. extra to all HMI examining more than 12,000 children a year.

1863 *Inspectors' Assistants* appointed; elementary head-teachers, assisting HMI with examining. Initially in urban areas.

1864 Lowe resigned on altering Report. Now fifty-nine HMI.

1867 Liberalizing of the curriculum, one or more 'specific subjects of secular instruction' allowed for grant purposes. More pressure on inspectors.

1869 Last clergyman appointed as HMI.

1870 Education Act.
End of 1840 Concordat.
HMI organized territorially into eight Divisions.
Religious instruction no longer inspected by HMI.

1880	Mundella's Elementary Education Act. New Code encouraged class teaching.
1881	Code Committee, consisting of three Education Department officials, three HMI and the Vice-President, established to consider amendments to the Code. New rank of *Sub-Inspector* created, to carry out many of the duties of an Inspector.
1882	Revised Code called for greater uniformity in Inspectors' standards. Annual divisional conferences of Inspectors reinstituted.
1883	First woman appointed, Miss Emily Jones, Directress of Needlework.
1886	Cross Commission on the Working of the Elementary Education Acts recommended that well-qualified men with elementary school experience should be recruited to the Inspectorate. Experiment to be tried of appointing women as Sub-Inspectresses in large towns to examine young children.
1890	*Revised Instructions* allowed HMI to 'sample' class work and pay more frequent 'visits without notice' to schools. Aimed at taking burden off HMI and giving more freedom to teachers and managers. First Senior Chief Inspector, Rev. T. W. Sharpe, appointed.
1891	Occasional visits substituted for examination in infants' schools.
1892	First ex-elementary school teacher, F. S. Marvin, appointed HMI.
1892	Hon. Mrs R. E. Colborne, successor to Miss Jones, first permanent woman appointment.
1895	Sub-Inspectors renamed *First Class Sub-Inspectors* and Inspectors' Assistants became *Second Class Sub-Inspectors*.
1896	First two women Sub-Inspectors appointed, Miss R.A. Munday and Miss S. J. Willis.
1898	Ending of 'payment by results' system.
1899	Board of Education Act. Central Authority for education, amalgamating the Education Department and the Science and Art Department.
1900	Recruitment of Sub-Inspectors, First and Second Class, ended.
1901	New grade of *Junior Inspector*, mainly for young

university graduates, established.

Twenty Inspectors from Science and Art Department became HMI.

1902   Education Act abolished School Boards. Local Education Authorities (LEAs) now exercised control over public education.

1903   Morant appointed as Permanent Secretary, Board of Education.

Board and Inspectorate divided into three branches: *Elementary*, *Secondary* and *Technological* with office staff arranged territorially corresponding to divisions.

Chief Inspectors appointed for each branch and a fourth for training institutions and Art Schools.

Divisional Inspectors, eleven in number, each in charge of a geographical division and responsible for all inspection in his area.

Chief Woman Inspector, Hon. Maude Lawrence, appointed.

First Board of Education Educational Pamphlet published.

1905   Women Inspectorate came into being, concerned mainly with cookery and inspection of young children.

Eleven Inspectors, given the title HMI (Women).

Publication of *Suggestions for the Consideration of Teachers and Others Concerned in the Work of Public Elementary Schools*, from 1927 called *Handbook of Suggestions for Teachers*; largely written by HMI.

The 'Full Inspection' developed by the Secondary Inspectorate.

1907   Separate Welsh Department established, with its own Chief Inspector, Owen M. Edwards.

1908   Both classes of Sub-Inspectors merged into one class called Sub-Inspector.

HMI and LEAs undertook system of area reports for technical education in their areas, taking three years.

Dr A. Eicholz, HMI, appointed as Medical Inspector.

1912   Royal Commission on the Civil Service recommended changes in the method of selection and appointment of HMI.

1913   New class of *Assistant Inspector*, for experienced teachers and those with other qualifications, established, with higher salary than *Sub-Inspectors*.

Area surveys of secondary education undertaken.

159

Appendix I

1919 Formation of the Board of Education Inspectors' Association.

First woman Staff Inspector, Miss A. E. Wark, appointed.

1921 Assistant Inspectors, Sub-Inspectors and remaining Junior Inspectors merged into one grade, *Assistant Inspectors*, with improved salary scale.

1922 Board of Education reorganized; separate Elementary, Secondary and Technological Branches abolished.

1926 Inspectorate reorganized into a unified body:

(i) The three Chief Inspectors, one of whom was the *Senior Chief Inspector* (SCI), acted as expert advisers to the Board. The Chief Woman Inspector also responsible to SCI.

(ii) Each of the nine Divisions now had one officer, the *Divisional Inspector* (DI), who linked together all forms of educational activity. Directly responsible to SCI.

(iii) Twelve *Staff Inspectors* (SI) made available to SCI for work in connection with the Department of Special Inquiries and Reports and in schools.

Reorganization completed by 1929.

Public advertising of HMI posts began.

1930 Post of Chief Medical Inspector ceased to exist.

1931 The Royal Commission on the Civil Service recommended that more women should by stages be incorporated into the main organization of the Inspectorate.

1933 First women District Inspectors, Elementary and Secondary Branches appointed.

1934 Men and women Inspectorates unified: given equal responsibilities

1936 First woman Divisional Inspector, Miss D. Hammonds, appointed.

1938 Title of Chief Woman Inspector replaced by Senior Woman Inspector.

1944 Education Act.

Departmental Committee of HMI and Board of Education officials set up to consider changes necessary.

(i) Inspectorate became fully unified body, not only at upper levels. Distinction between Elementary and Secondary Branches of Inspectorate abolished. The Women Inspectors ceased to operate as a separate body.

(ii) There were now six Chief Inspectors instead of three, with a separately appointed Senior Chief Inspector, (Martin Roseveare).

(iii) The post of Divisional Inspector gained status, becoming more concerned with educational than administrative matters (ten Divisions now).

(iv) The grade of Assistant Inspector was abolished.

(v) Increase in size of Inspectorate as a result of widening range of duties arising from 1944 Education Act. In 1949, there were 527 HMI.

1947 First woman Chief Inspector, Miss F. M. Tann, appointed.

1961 Equal pay for men and women Inspectors achieved.

1962 A Curriculum Study Group was set up by the Minister of Education, David Eccles. It consisted of HMI, officials and a university educationist, and was asked to give urgent advice on the school curriculum.

1964 Schools Council for Curriculum and Examinations established. HMI involved in work of the Council.

1968 Select Committee on Education and Science investigated the role of HMI. Recommended that as a general rule full-scale formal inspections should be discontinued.

1974 Assessment of Performance Unit (APU) set up, with HMI involvement. First woman Senior Chief Inspector, Sheila Browne, appointed.

1976 James Callaghan initiates the 'Great Debate' in Ruskin College speech. (Oct.)
'Yellow Book' leaked. (July)

1977 *Education in Schools. A Consultative Document.*
Curriculum 11 to 16, an HMI discussion document.

1978 National survey by HMI published, *Primary Education in England*.

1979 National survey by HMI published, *Aspects of Secondary Education in England*.

1980 Terms of reference of Sir Derek Rayner's study on the role, organization, staffing and effectiveness of HMI in England and Wales published.
A View of the Curriculum, an HMI document, issued.

1981 Inspection of initial teacher training courses in university departments of education began.
Evidence by HMI to House of Commons Education, Science and Arts Committee on the Secondary School

Curriculum and Examinations 14 to 16.

First publication of HMI report, *On the Effects on the Education Service in England of Local Authority Expenditure Policies.*

1982   *Education 5–9* and DES paper *The School Curriculum* published.

1983   *Study of HM Inspectorate in England and Wales* (Rayner Report) favourable to HMI.

HMI reports on schools and colleges published. *The Work of HM Inspectorate in England and Wales* and *HM Inspectors Today: Standards in Education. Curriculum 11 to 16: Towards a Statement of Entitlement. 9 to 13: An Illustrative Survey. Teaching Quality* and *Education Observed* issued.

1984   CATE established.

1985   *Better Schools, Curriculum 5–16* and *Education 8 to 12 in combined and Middle Schools: an HMI Survey* published.

1986   *Better Schools Evaluation and Appraisal Conference Birmingham* November 1985 published.

Reporting Inspections: HMI Methods and Procedures. Three booklets explaining how inspections are carried out in maintained schools, independent schools and further and higher education institutions.

Appendix II

Numbers of HMI (1839–1985)

The following table refers to the English Inspectorate only. Firm numbers are often not possible as not all sources uniformly include grades other than full HMI, i.e., Assistant Inspectors, Inspectors' Assistants, Sub-Inspectors, Junior Inspectors, Women Inspectors and Science and Art Department Inspectors.

1839 – 2	1915 – 350
1845 – 5	1920 – 395
1850 – 17	1925 – 324
1855 – 24	1930 – 307
1860 – 48	1935 – 319
1865 – 67	1940 – 329
1870 – 92	1945 – 364
1875 – 104	1950 – 565
1880 – 269	1955 – 500
1885 – 303	1960 – 475
1890 – 301	1965 – 543
1895 – 322	1970 – 483
1900 – 349	1975 – 430
1905 – 334	1980 – 421
1910 – 336	1985 – 490

Appendix III

Department of Education and Science

Organization at January 1985

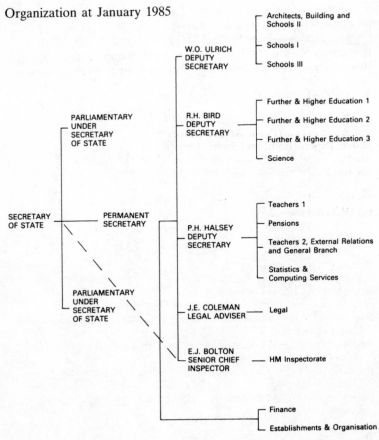

Bibliography

A Archive sources
B Official reports
C Books and pamphlets
D Articles

A Archive sources

Crewe Papers (Cambridge University Library)
Education Papers (Public Record Office)
Marvin Papers (Bodleian Library, Oxford)
Runciman Papers (Newcastle upon Tyne University Library)
Spencer Papers (British Library)

B Official reports

Royal Commissions

Report of the Commissioners Appointed to Enquire into the State of
  Popular Education in England (Newcastle Commission) 1861
Reports of the Royal Commission on Scientific Instruction and the
  Advancement of Science (Devonshire Commission) 1872–5
Reports of the Royal Commission on Technical Instruction (Samuelson
  Commission) 1882–4
Reports of the Royal Commission on the Elementary Education Acts
  (Cross Commission) 1886–8
Report of the Royal Commission on Secondary Education (Bryce
  Commission) 1895
Report of the Royal Commission on the Civil Service (MacDonnell
  Commission) 1912–13

Bibliography

Report of the Royal Commission on the Civil Service 1930–1
Report of the Royal Commission on the Civil Service 1953:

Board of Education (HMSO unless otherwise stated)

General Reports on Higher Education (1902). 'Report on the Teaching
   of Literacy in Some Secondary Schools' by J. W. Headlam
*Reports on Children under Five Years of Age in Public Elementary
   Schools* (1905)
*Suggestions for the Consideration of Teachers and Others Concerned with
   the work of Public Elementary Schools* (1905). (From 1927 renamed
   Handbook of Suggestions for Teachers)
Circular 705 *Memorandum on Language Teaching in State-Aided
   Secondary Schools in England* (1909)
Educational Pamphlet No. 24 *The Montessori System of Education*
   (1912)
Annual Report 1922–3 (1924)
Circular 1382 *Reorganisation of the Board's Inspectorate (England)* 21
   July 1926
Hadow Report, Report of the Consultative Committee on *The
   Education of the Adolescent* (1926).
Educational Pamphlet No. 63 *Memorandum on Examinations for
   Scholarships and Free Places in Secondary Schools* (1928)
Hadow Report, Report of the Consultative Committee on *The Primary
   School* (1931)
Educational Pamphlet No. 91 *Trades Schools on the Continent* (1932)
Hadow Report, Report of the Consultative Committee on *Infant and
   Nursery Schools* (1933)
Educational Pamphlet No. 110 *Homework* (1937a)
Co-operation in Technical Education (1937b)
Green Book *Education After the War* (1941)
Norwood Report, *Curriculum and Examinations in Secondary Schools:
   Report of the Committee of the Secondary School Examinations
   Council* (1943)
White Paper *Educational Reconstruction* (1943)
McNair Report *The Supply, Recruitment and Training of Teachers and
   Youth Leaders* (1944)

Ministry of Education

Education in 1949 (1950)
White Paper *Technical Education* (1956)
Jackson Report, *The Supply and Training of Teachers for Technical
   Colleges* (1957)
White Paper *Secondary Education for All: a new drive* (1958)

Primary Education (1959)
CACE *15 to 18* (Crowther Report) (1959)
White Paper *Better Opportunities in Technical Education* (1961)

Department of Education and Science

Lockwood Report, *Working Party on Schools Curricula and Examinations* (1964)
White Paper *A Plan for Polytechnics and other Colleges* (1966)
Plowden Report, Report of the CACE on *Children and Their Primary Schools* (1967)
HMI Today and Tomorrow (1970)
Open Plan Primary Schools. Education Survey 16 (1972a)
James Report, *Teacher Education and Training* (1972b)
White Paper, *Education: A Framework for Expansion* (1972c)
Circular 7/73
Bullock Report, *A Language for Life* (1975)
Green Paper *Education in Schools: A Consultative Document* (1977a)
Circular 14/77, *Local Authority Arrangements for the School Curriculum* (1977b)
Educating Our Children: Four subjects for Debate (1977c)
Curriculum 11 to 16 (1977d)
Primary Education in England: A Survey by HMI (1978)
Management Review of the DES 1977–8 (1979a)
Aspects of Secondary Education in England: A Survey by HMI (1979b)
Local Authority Arrangements for the School Curriculum (1979c)
Framework for the School Curriculum (1980a)
A View of the Curriculum (1980b)
The School Curriculum (1981a)
Report by HMI on the Effects of Local Authority Expenditure Policies on Education Provision in England (1981b)
Curriculum 11 to 16: A Review of Progress (1981c)
The New Teacher in School (1982a)
Education 5 to 9: An Illustrative Survey (1982b)
9 to 13 Middle Schools: An Illustrative Survey (1983a)
Teaching Quality (1983b)
HM Inspectorate Today: Standards in Education (1983c)
Publication and Follow-up of HMI Reports (Administrative Memorandum 2/83) (1983d)
The Work of HM Inspectorate in England and Wales: A Policy Statement by the Secretary of State for Education and Science and the Secretary of State for Wales (1983e)
Curriculum 11 to 16: Towards a Statement of Entitlement (1983f)
Rayner Report, *Study of HM Inspectorate in England and Wales* (1983g)
Education Observed 1: A Review of the First Six Months of Published Reports of HMI (1984a)

Bibliography

Education Observed 2: A Review of Published Reports by HMI on Primary Schools and 11 to 16 and 12 to 16 Comprehensive Schools (1984b)
Education 8 to 12 in Combined and Middle Schools: An HMI Survey (1985a)
Education Observed 3: Good Teachers (1985b)
The Curriculum from 5 to 16 (1985c) (Curriculum Matters 2)
Better Schools. Evaluation and Appraisal Conference, Birmingham, 14–15 November 1985 (1986a)
Reporting Inspections: HMI Methods and Procedures (1986b)
  1. *Maintained Schools (1986)*
  2. *Independent Schools (1986)*
  3. *Further and Higher Education Institutions (1986)*

Annual Reports

Other official reports

Barlow Report, Committee appointed by the Lord President of the Council on *Scientific Manpower* (1946).
Robbins Report, Committee appointed by the Prime Minister on *Higher Education* (1963).
Select Committee on Education and Science (1967–8), 2 vols, Part 1 *HM Inspectorate* (England and Wales) (1968).
House of Commons *Tenth Report from the Expenditure Committee Session 1975–6, Policy Making in the DES* (1976)
House of Commons *Second Report from the Education, Science and Arts Committee. The Secondary Schools Curriculum and Examinations with Special Reference to the 14 to 16 Year Old Group* (2 vols 1981)
House of Commons *Education, Science and Arts Committee, Achievement in Primary Schools. Minutes of Evidence 1984–5* (1985)
Audit Commission Report (1985), *Towards Better Management of Secondary Education*

Department of Employment

A Better Start in Working Life (1979)

Further Education (Curriculum Review and Development) Unit (FEU)

A Basis for Choice (1979) FEU
Vocational Preparation (1981) FEU

Manpower Services Commission (MSC)

Towards a Comprehensive Manpower Policy (1976) MSC
Young People and Work (1977) MSC
A New Training Initiative: An Agenda for Action (1981) MSC

Organization for Economic Co-operation and Development (OECD)

Educational Development Strategy in England and Wales (1975), OECD,
    Paris.

Schools Council

Working Paper 33: *Choosing a Curriculum for the Young School Leaver*
    (1971).
Working Paper 53: *The Whole Curriculum 13 to 16* (1975), Evans/
    Methuen.
Working Paper 55: *The Curriculum in the Middle Years* (1975), Evans/
    Methuen.

C   Books and pamphlets

Adams, J. W. (ed.) (1924), *Educational Movements and Methods*,
    Harrap.
Allen, B. M. (1934), *Sir Robert Morant*, Macmillan.
Association of HMs Inspectors of Schools (1954), *Memorandum
    Submitted by the Association, 1 July 1954, to the Royal Commission on
    the Civil Service, 1954*, HMSO.
Ball, N. (1963), *Her Majesty's Inspectorate 1839–1849*, Oliver Boyd.
Banks, O. (1955), *Parity and Prestige in English Secondary Education*,
    Routledge & Kegan Paul.
Bishop, A. S. (1971), *The Rise of a Central Authority for English
    Education*, Cambridge University Press.
Blackie, J. (1970), *Inspecting and the Inspectorate*, Routledge & Kegan
    Paul.
Boothroyd, H. E. (1923), *A History of the Inspectorate*, Board of
    Education Inspectors' Association
Boyle, E. and Crosland, A. (1971), *The Politics of Education*, Penguin.
Burrows, L. J. (1978), *The Middle School – High Road or Dead-end?*,
    Woburn Press.
Christian, G. A. (1922), *English Education from Within*, Wallace
    Gandy.
Clark, L. (1976), *The Inspector Remembers*, Dobson.

Cox, C. B. and Dyson, A. E. (eds) (1969), *Fight for Education: A Black Paper*, London Critical Quarterly Society.

Dunford, J. E. (1980), *Her Majesty's Inspectorate of Schools in England and Wales, 1860–1870*, Monograph no. 9, University of Leeds.

Eaglesham, E. J. R. (1953), *The Foundations of Twentieth Century Education in England*, Routledge & Kegan Paul.

Edmonds, E. L. (1962), *The School Inspector*, Routledge & Kegan Paul.

Edmonds, E. L. and Edmonds, O. P. (eds) (1965), *I Was There. The Memoirs of H. S. Tremenheere*, Shakespeare Head Press, Eton, Windsor.

Elton, E. A. (1974), *Secondary Education in the East Riding of Yorkshire 1944–1974*, Educational Administration and History Monograph no. 2, University of Leeds.

Evans, K. (1975), *The Development and Structure of the English Education System*, Hodder & Stoughton.

Evans, K. (1985), *The Development and Structure of the English School System*, Hodder & Stoughton.

Fearon, D. R. (1876), *School Inspection*, Macmillan.

Fenwick, I. G. K. (1976), *The Comprehensive School 1944–1970*, Methuen.

Fisher, P. (1982), *External Examinations in Secondary Schools in England and Wales 1944–1964*, Educational Administration and History Monograph No. 11, University of Leeds.

Fitch, J. (1897), *Thomas and Matthew Arnold and Their Influence on English Education*, Heinemann.

Gosden, P. H. J. H. (1966), *The Development of Educational Administration in England and Wales*, Blackwell.

Gosden, P. H. J. H. (1976), *Education In the Second World War: A Study in Policy and Administration*, Methuen.

Gosden, P. H. J. H. (1983), *The Education System Since 1944*, Martin Robertson.

Gretton, J. and Jackson, M. (1976), *William Tyndale, Collapse of a School – or a System?* Allen & Unwin.

Grier, L. (1952), *Achievement in Education. The Work of Michael Ernest Sadler 1885–1935*, Constable.

Holmes, E. (1911), *What Is and What Might Be*, Constable.

Hurt, J. S. (1979), *Elementary Schooling and the Working Classes 1860–1918*, Routledge & Kegan Paul.

ILEA (1976), *William Tyndale Junior and Infants Schools. Public Inquiry. A Report to the ILEA by Robin Auld, Q.C.*, ILEA.

Kogan, M. (1971), *The Politics of Educational Change*, Fontana/Collins.

Kogan, M. and Packwood, T. (1974), *Advisory Councils and Committees in Education*, Routledge & Kegan Paul.

Kogan, M. (1986), *Education Accountability*, Hutchinson.

Lawton, D. (1980), *The Politics of the School Curriculum*, Routledge & Kegan Paul.

Lawton, D. (1984), *The Tightening Grip*, University of London Institute of Education, Bedford Way Papers 21.

Leese, J. (1950), *Personalities and Power in English Education*, Arnold.

Lowndes, G. A. N. (1937), *The Silent Social Revolution*, Oxford University Press.

Maclure, S. (1970), *One Hundred Years of London Education 1870–1970*, Allen Lane, Penguin.

Maud, J. Baron Redcliffe-Maud (1981), *Experiences of an Optimist*, Hamish Hamilton.

Niblett, W. R. *et al.* (1975), *The University Connection*, NFER.

OECD (1976), *Report on Britain*, reprinted in Raggatt, R. *et al.* (1977), *The Political Context*, Ward Lock.

Pankhurst, E. (1914), *My Own Story*, Eveleigh Nash.

Parkin, G. R. (1898), *Life and Letters of Edward Thring*, 2 vols, Macmillan.

Peters, R. S. (ed.) (1969), *Perspectives on Plowden*, Routledge & Kegan Paul.

Pile, W. (1979), *The Department of Education and Science*, Allen & Unwin.

Potter, F. F. (1949), *Educational Journey: Memories of Fifty Years in Public Education*, Pitman.

Raymont, T. (1934), *Modern Education: Its Aims and Methods*, Longmans, Green.

Rhodes, G. (1981), *Inspectorates in British Government*, Allen & Unwin.

Salter, B., and Tapper, T. (1981), *Education, Politics and the State*, Grant McIntyre.

Selleck, R. J. W. (1968), *The New Education. The English Background*, Pitman.

Selleck, R. J. W. (1972), *English Primary Education and the Progressives*, Routledge & Kegan Paul.

Sherington, G. (1981), *English Education, Social Change and War 1911–20*, Methuen.

Sillitoe, H. (1933), *A History of the Teaching of Domestic Subjects*, Methuen.

Smith, F. (1923), *Life of Sir James Kay-Shuttleworth*, John Murray.

Sneyd-Kynnersley, E. M. (1908), *Some Passages in the Life of One of HM Inspectors of Schools*, Macmillan.

Spencer, F. H. (1938), *An Inspector's Testament*, English University Press.

Squire, R. E. (1927), *Thirty Years in the Public Service*, Nisbet.

Sturt, M. (1967), *The Education of the People*, Routledge & Kegan Paul.

Sutherland, G. (1973), *Policy-Making in Elementary Education 1870–1895*, Oxford University Press.

Swinburne, A. J. (1912), *Memories of a School Inspector*, privately published.

Sykes, T. P. (1911), *Function and Position of HM Inspectors of Schools in the Elementary School System*, paper read at NUT Conference, Aberystwyth, 1911, NUT.

171

Sylvester, D. W. (1974), *Robert Lowe and Education*, Cambridge University Press.
Taylor, W. (1963), *The Secondary Modern School*, Faber & Faber.
Turnbull, H. W. (1919), *Some Memories of William Peveril Turnbull, one of His Majesty's Inspectors of Schools*, Bell.
Vernon, B. D. (1982), *Ellen Wilkinson*, Croom Helm.
Whitbread, N. (1972), *The Evolution of the Nursery-Infant School*, Routledge & Kegan Paul.
Wilson, P. (1961), *Views and Prospects from Curzon Street: Seven Essays and Addresses on the Future of Education*, Blackwell.

D   Articles

Armytage, W. H. G. (1950) 'J. F. D. Donnelly: Pioneer in Vocational Education', *Vocational Aspects of Secondary and Further Education*, vol. 2, no. 4.
Bartle, G. F. (1984), 'The Agents and Inspectors of the British and Foreign School Society, 1826–84', *History of Education Society Bulletin*, no. 34, Autumn.
Bolton, E. (1983), 'The Inspector Inspected', *Report (AMMA Journal)*, vol. 6, no. 3, Nov.
Boyle, Lord (1972), 'The Politics of Secondary School Reorganisation: Some Reflections', *Journal of Educational Administration and History*, vol. 4, no.2.
Briault, E. (1976), 'A Distributed System of Educational Administration: an International Viewpoint', *International Review of Education*, vol. 22, no. 4, pp. 429–39.
Browne, S. (1977), 'Curriculum: an HMI view', *Trends in Education*, no. 3, HMSO.
Drake, K. (1976), 'Educational Planning by Halves', *Higher Education Review*, vol. 9. no. 1.
Dunford, J. E. (1981), 'Biographical Details of Her Majesty's Inspectors Appointed Before 1870', *History of Education Society Bulletin*, no. 28, Autumn.
Goldstein, H. and Blinkhorn, S. (1977), 'Monitoring Educational Standards. An Inappropriate Model', *Bulletin of the British Psychological Society*, vol. 30, Sep.
Gordon, P. (1978), 'Edith Mary Deverell: An Early Woman Inspector', *History of Education Society Bulletin*, no. 22, Autumn.
Gordon, P. (1980), 'Homework. Origins and Justifications', *Westminster Studies in Education*, vol. iii.
Gordon, P. (1985), 'The Handbook of Suggestions for Teachers', *Journal of Educational Administration and History*, vol. 17, no. 1.
Kay, B. W. (1975), 'Monitoring Pupils' Performance', *Trends in Education*, no. 2, HMSO.
Musgrave, P. (1970), 'Constant Factors in the Demand for Technical

Education 1860–1960', in Musgrave, P. (ed.), *Sociology, History and Education*, Methuen.

Szreter, R. (1964), 'The Origin of Full-time Compulsory Education at Five', *British Journal of Educational Studies*, vol. 13, no. 1.

Wallace, R. G. (1981), 'The Origins and Authorship of the 1944 Education Act', *History of Education*, vol. 10, no. 4.

Wilson, P. (1964) 'Inspecting the Inspectorate', *Twentieth Century*, Spring.

Index

Abbott, A., 70

Acland, A.H.D., 16, 86, 124

Acts: Board of Education (1899), 49; Education (1870), 12, 31, 157; (1880), 158; (1902), 17, 18, 49, 75; (1921); 129, (1944), 22, 31, 60, 72, 78, 102, 130; Elementary Education (Blind and Deaf Children) (1893), 19; Employment and Training (1973), 73; Endowed Schools (1869), 48; Industrial Training (1964), 73; Local Taxation (Customs and Excise) (1890), 16, 88; Technical Instruction (1889), 15, 16, 88

Adams, John, 37

Adderley, C.B., 10, 156

Advisory Committee on the Supply and Education of Teachers (ACSET), 152

Allen, J., 8, 156

Althorp, Lord, 7

Andrew, Sir Herbert, 106–7, 114

Anson, Sir William, 33

Arnold, Matthew, 10, 12, 30

Asquith, H.H., 88

Assessment of Performance Unit (APU), 153–4, 161

Auld, Robin, 42

Barlow Report (1946), 72

Barnett, P.A., 50

B.Ed. degree, 82–3

Beloe Report (1960), 130–1

Bergman, Martina, 87

Bernstein, Basil, 41

Biggs, Edith, 39

Black Papers, 40, 105

Blair, Sir Robert, 42

Blandford, J.J., 10

Board of Education, 17–19, 32–5, 37–8, 49–52, 56, 69–71, 103, 115–16, 129

Bolton, Eric, 135–8, 148

Booth, Clive, 123

Boothroyd, H.E., 13, 116

Boyle, Sir Edward, 25–6, 61, 132

Blackie, J.H., 115

Briault, E., 109, 112

British and Foreign School Society, 8, 156

Browne, Sheila, 27–8, 74, 107, 117–18, 134–5, 137–9, 161

Bryce Report (1895), 53

Buckmaster, C.A., 69, 128

Bullock Report (1975), 29

Burnham, Lord, 75

Burt, Cyril, 58

Butler, R.A., 78, 80

Callaghan, James, 27, 111, 161

Cecil, Lord Robert, 11

Certificate of Pre-Vocational Education (CPVE), 74

Chambers, Edmund, 75

City and Guilds of London Institute, 49, 68–9, 71, 106, 139

Civil Service, Royal Commission on: (1912–13), 96, 103, 159; (1929–30), 97, 123, 160

Clark, Leonard, 122

Clifford, Miss M., 93

Colborne, Hon. Mrs. R.E., 158

Cole, Sir Henry, 15

Committee of the Privy Council on Education, 8, 10, 15–16, 31, 103, 156

Cook, F.C., 156

Coulton, G.C., 50

Council for National Academic Awards (CNAA), 73

Council for the Accreditation of Teacher Education (CATE), 84, 149

Cranbrook, Lord, 127

Crewe, Lord, 124

Crosby, Miss A.D., 93

Crosland, Anthony, 61

Cross Report (1888), 75, 158

Crowther Report (1959), 72

Curriculum Study Group, 107, 161

Dale, F.B., 42

Dalton, J.E., 71

Dalton Plan, 37

Davies, Brian, 41

Davies, W.R., 33

Dearden, Robert, 40

Degani, Miss M.A., 93

Department of Education and Science (DES): 1–4, 26–7, 62–5, 74, 80–3, 99–100, 104, 106–7, 109–14, 123–5, 133–4, 141, 144–7, 151–5; Department Planning Organization (DPO), 26, 133; Joint Planning Committee, 133; Planning Branch, 26, 133; Policy Group for Inspection (PGI), 145; Policy Steering Group (PSG), 26, 133; Programme Analysis and Research (PAR), 26; *see also* Her Majesty's Inspectorate

Department of Employment, 154

Deverell, Miss Edith, M. (later Mrs Marvin), 89, 91, 93

Devonshire, 7th Duke of, 67

Devonshire, 8th Duke of, 17, 49, 116

Donnelly, J.F.D., 15, 67–8

Duckworth, F.R.G., 42, 129, 137–8

Eccles, Sir David, 130, 161

Edmonds, E.L., 102–3, 125–6

Education Department, 11, 15, 17, 31–2, 127

Education, Science and Arts Committee, House of Commons: *Secondary Curriculum and Examinations 14–16* (1981), 134–5, 162; *Achievement in Primary Schools* (1984–5), 135–6

Edwards, Owen, M., 159

Eicholz, Alfred, 19, 33, 159

'Eleven Plus' tests, 58–60

Elliott, W.R., 99, 132–3, 137–8

Elvin, Lionel, 40, 82

Emergency Training Scheme, 81

English, Cyril, 106, 131–2, 138–9

Fawcett, Philippa, 91

Feilden, R.R., 102, 107

Finny, A.J., 116–17

Fisher, H.A.L., 94, 98, 119

Fleming Report (1944), 129

Fletcher, William Charles, 50, 54, 56–8, 94

Forster, W.E., 86

Foss, Brian, 40

Free Place Regulations (1907), 58

French, H.W., 27, 133–4, 137–9

Further Education Unit (FEU), 74

Index

Garrett, Elizabeth, 87

Goodenough, Sir F., 71

Gorst, Sir John, 89

'Great Debate' (1976), 27, 43, 109, 161

Hadow Reports: (1926) *The Education of the Adolescent*, 37; (1931) *The Primary School*, 37; (1933) *Infant and Nursery Schools*, 37

Hammonds, Miss D.M., 22, 99, 160

Handbook of Suggestions see Official Publications

Harrison, Miss Mary, 88

Hard Times, 30

Headlam, J.W., 53

Heath, Frank, 33

Her Majesty's Inspectorate (HMI): appointment, 115; attitude to Revised Code, 11–13; attitude to teachers, 13, 34–6; curriculum, 27–8, 62–4, 108, 153; early social composition, 9–10; future of, 149–55; interchange with Office, 124–5; interchange with teaching, 125–6; medical aspects, 18–19; origins, 7–8, 116; political pressure on, 5, 111, 151, 155; publication of reports, 6, 135–6, 162; Rayner analysis and recommendations, 141–9; reorganization (1903), 17–18, 50, (1926), 129, (1944), 23; structure, 2–3; work of HMIs, 4–6, 8–10, 120–2

Elementary/Primary Inspection changing methods of working, 46–7; ending of 'payment by results', 31–2; enlightened philosophy, 36–9; *Handbook of Suggestions*, 32–4; middle schools, 41–2, 45–7; reaction to Plowden, 39–41; timetable approval, 35–6

Further and Higher Education Inspection duties, 18, 69–74; universities and teacher training, 74–85

Secondary Inspection attitudes to comprehensive education, 24, 60–2; attitudes to 'eleven plus', 58–60; curriculum, 62–4; establishment of Secondary Inspectorate, 50–1; examinations and homework, 57–8; full inspection and alternatives, 51–6; origins, 48–50; relations with LEAs, 64–5

HMI and DES changing relation with, 26–7, 104–14; comprehensivization, 61; differences on curriculum, 63; HMI independence of, 25, 103–4, 151, 155; interchange between HMI and Office, 123–5; Rayner Report and closer co-operation, 145–7; teacher education and universities, 80–1

HMI and LEAs annual reviews of LEA expenditure, 5, 29, 134, 147–8, 162; contacts with LEAs, 3–5; different functions from LEA advisers, 1, 105–6, 122, 143, 154; early Women Inspectors, 92; effect of 'eleven plus', 58–60; effect of Local Government Act (1972), 45, 108; comprehensive schemes, 61; curriculum experiments in, 64, 144; HMI relations with LEAs and DES, 109–11; Holmes-Morant Circular, 34–5; inspection of LEAs, 122, 149, 153; Rayner recommendations, 147

Women Inspectors aggregation, 97–8; creation and functions of Women Inspectorate, 90–6; equal pay issue, 98–9; imbalance in numbers between men and women, 100–1; origins, 86–8

Hogg, Quintin, 68

Holmes, Edmond, 20, 34–7

Holmes-Morant Circular, 34–5

Holmes, Sir Maurice, 42, 124

Homework, 57–8

Hudson, J.A., 133

Inner London Education Authority (ILEA), 144

Interdepartmental Committee on Physical Deterioration (1904), 91

Jackson, Cyril, 33, 92, 128

Jackson Report (1957), 72

James Report (1972), 83

Jeffrey, G.B., 81, 84

Jones, Miss Emily, 88, 158

Jones, Stephen, 123

Joseph, Sir Keith, 84, 136, 148

Kay-Shuttleworth, Sir James, 8, 10, 74, 103, 126, 156

Kekewich, Sir George, 116, 127–8

King, T., 128, 137–8

Kogan, Maurice, 25, 61, 106

Lansdowne, Lord, 10

Larkrise to Candleford, 30

Lawrence, Hon. Maude, 87, 91–2, 159

Lawrence, Lord, 91

Leese, John, 50, 52, 69

Leigh, Lady, 86

Lindsell, H.M., 124

Lloyd, Geoffrey, 60–1

Lloyd, W.Ll., 133

Local Education Authorities (LEAs), 1, 4–5, 24, 29, 33, 35–7, 42, 45, 47, 49–50, 53, 55, 58–9, 61, 64, 72, 83, 92–3, 95, 97–8, 105–14, 123, 125, 142–5, 147–50, 153–5; *see also* Her Majesty's Inspectorate

London County Council (LCC), 42, 98, 119

London School Board, 30

London Technical Education Board, 68

Lowe, Robert, 10–11, 103, 157

McMillan, Margaret, 36

McNair Report (1944), 78–81

Mack, Jennie, 39

Malcolm Report (1928), 71

Manpower Services Commission (MSC), 73, 154

Marshall, Miss M.J., 100

Marshall, T.W., 156

Marvin, F.S., 89, 158

Maud, John, 23

Maud Report (1969), 108

Mayor, M., 76

Ministry of Education, 23, 38–9, 60, 72, 80–1, 109

Monkhouse, Miss R.L., 76

Morant, R.L., 17, 32, 35, 50, 90–1, 101, 116, 124, 159

Morrell, J.D., 156

Montessori, Maria, 36

Mulley, Fred, 27

Munday, Miss R.A., 89, 158

National Foundation for Educational Research (NFER), 43

National Society, 8, 156

National Union of Teachers (NUT), 35–6, 77, 105

Newcastle Report (1861), 11, 157

New Code (1882), 32, 88, 158

New Education Fellowship, 37

Newsom Report (1963), 62

Niblett, W.R., 77

Norwood, Cyril, 57

Norwood Report (1943), 60, 117, 125, 126

Nunn, Percy, 37

Oakden, Miss E.C. (later Mrs Mee), 78–80

Official Publications:
A Basis for Choice (1979), 74
A Better Start in Working Life (1980), 73
A Framework for the School Curriculum (1980), 63, 110
A New Training Initiative. An Agenda for Action (1981), 74
A Plan for Polytechnics and Other Colleges (1966), 73
Aspects of Secondary Education in England (1979), 29, 63, 84, 143, 161

Index

A View of the Curriculum (1980), 63, 110, 161

Better Opportunities in Technical Education (1961), 73

Circular 10/1965, 45, 61

Circular 7/1973, 83

Circular 14/1977, 109

Co-operation in Technical Education (1937), 71

Curriculum 11–16 (Red Book) (1977), 27–8, 62, 144, 161

Curriculum 11–16. A Review of Progress (1981), 64

Curriculum 11–16. Towards a Statement of Entitlement (1983), 28, 61, 162

Curriculum Matters (1984–5), 28, 111, 136, 153

Curriculum 5–16 (1985), 44

Educating our Children (1977), 43

Education 5 to 9 (1982), 44

Education: a Framework for Expansion (1973), 83

Education after the War (Green Book), (1941), 22, 77–8

Education in Schools. A Consultative Document (Green Paper) (1977), 62, 109, 161

Education 8 to 12 in Combined and Middle Schools (1985), 46–7, 162

Education Observed (1983), 65

Educational Reconstruction (1943), 78

Effects of Local Authority Expenditure Policies on Education Provision in England (1981), 5, 29, 134, 147–8, 162

Handbook of Suggestions (1905–37), 19, 32, 36–7, 53, 62, 159

HMI Today and Tomorrow (1970), 126

HMI Today: Standards in Education (1983), 145, 161

Launching Middle Schools (1970), 45

Local Authority Arrangements for the School Curriculum (1979), 64

9–13 Middle Schools. An Illustrative Survey (1983), 46–7

Open Plan Primary Schools (1972), 41

Primary Education (1959), 38

Primary Education in England (1978), 29, 43–4, 84, 143, 161

Promoting Curriculum Innovation (1982), 74

Rayner Report (1983), 29, 74, 103–4, 132, 134, 141–9, 155, 161, 162

Reporting Inspections (1986), 52, 162

Reports on Children Under Five Years of Age (1905), 92

Secondary Education For All (1958), 45, 61

Secondary School Regulations (1903), 53; (1905), 50; (1907), 50, 56

Teaching Quality (1983), 84

Technical Education (1956), 72

Tenth Expenditure Committee, House of Commons. *Policy-Making in the DES* (1976), 133–4

The New Teacher in School (1982), 84

The School Curriculum (1982), 63, 110

The Work of HMI in England and Wales (1983), 104, 162

Towards a Comprehensive Manpower Policy (1976), 73

Towards Better Management of Secondary Education (1986), 111

Towards the Middle School (1970), 45

Young People at Work (1977), 73

Oppé, A.P., 76

Organization for Economic Co-operation and Development (OECD), 26–7, 109

Pankhurst, Emmeline, 87

Partington, Miss J., 141

Payment by Results, *see* Revised Code (1862)

Pedley, R.R., 100

Percy, Lord Eustace, 71–2, 77

Perry, Pauline, 123

Perspectives on Plowden, 40–1

Peters, R., 40

Philip, Miss A.G., 99

Phipps, Sir E., 116, 124

Pile, Sir William, 26, 133–4

Playfair, Lyon, 15

Plowden Report (1967), 23, 39–41, 43, 45, 83, 105–6

Potter, F.F., 119

Pullinger, F., 69, 70

Rate Support Grant (RSG), 110–11

Rayner, Sir Derek, 141

Rayner Report *see* Official Publications

Redgrave, Gilbert, 128

Regional Advisory Councils (RAC), 72

Revised Code (1862), 'Payment by Results', 11–13, 15, 30, 86, 103, 120, 157

Richards, Sir H.M., 76, 95–6, 129, 137–9

Robbins Report (1963), 73, 82

Roebuck, John, 7

Rooper, T.G., 33

Rose, Jim, 44

Roseveare Report (1956), 24, 108

Roseveare, Sir Martin, 24, 130–1, 137–9

Runciman, Walter, 34–5, 103

Sadler, Michael, 37, 49

Salter, B. and Tapper, T., 112–13

Samuelson Report (1884), 15, 67

Sandon, Lord, 13

Savage, E.G., 57–8, 129, 137–9

Schiller, Christian, 39

School Certificate Examination, 57

Schools Council for Curriculum and Examinations, 27, 61, 107–8, 131, 161

Science and Art Department, 14–17, 49, 66–7, 88, 115, 128, 156

Scott, R.P., 51

Scottish Education Department (SED) and HMI, 3, 155

Selby-Bigge, Sir L.A., 35–6, 75, 94, 103, 123

Select Committee on Education (1864), 103

Select Committee on Education and Science (1967–8), 24–5, 103, 105, 106, 107, 124–5, 132, 161

Senior Chief Inspector (SCI): backgrounds and careers, 137–40; duties, 2–3; history and development of post, 127–36

Senior, Mrs Jane Elizabeth, 88

Sharpe, T.W., 128, 137–9, 158

Sidgwick, Arthur, 50

Sillitoe, Miss Helen, 93

Sneyd-Kynnersley, E.M., 121

South Kensington Inspectorate, 14–17, 67–9

Spencer, F., 51

Spencer, F.H., 119

Spencer, Lord, 88

Spens Report (1938), 60

Squire, Miss R.E., 89

Stead, F.B., 51

Stuart, N.W., 141

Sykes, T.P., 36

Symonds, Sir A.V., 119

Tann, Miss F.M., 99, 161

Tanner, Robin, 39

Technical and Vocational Education Initiative (TVEI), 74, 155

Thatcher, Margaret, 29, 83, 111, 141

Thomson, Godfrey, 58

Thring, Edward, 48

Tremenheere, H.S., 8, 10, 156

Trenaman Report (1981), 110

Turnbull, W.P., 30

Universities Council for the Education of Teachers (UCET), 84

Vidal, Miss H.E., 100

Index

Ward, Herbert, 75
Wark, Miss A.E., 94–5, 160
Watson, Foster, 50
Watts, A.F., 59
Weaver, T.R., 82
Welsh Office, 3, 133, 141–2
Wilkinson, Ellen, 80–1
William Tyndale School, London, 41–2
Williams, G.G., 22
Williams, Shirley, 123
Willis, Miss S.J., 89, 158

Wilson, Percy, 24, 130–1, 138
Women Inspectors *see* Her Majesty's
  Inspectorate
Wood, R.S., 22–3, 116
Wood, S.H., 22, 78–81

Yellow Book (1976), 27, 109, 161
Youth Opportunities Programme
  (YOP), 73
Youth Training Scheme (YTS), 74,
  135–6